YOUNG ADULT POETRY

YOUNG ADULT POETRY

A Survey and Theme Guide

Rachel Schwedt and Janice DeLong
Foreword by Mel Glenn

GREENWOOD PRESS

Westport, Connecticut • London

Library of Congress Cataloging-in-Publication Data

Schwedt, Rachel E., 1944–
    Young adult poetry : a survey and theme guide / Rachel Schwedt and Janice DeLong ;
    foreword by Mel Glenn.
        p.   cm.
    Includes indexes.
    ISBN 0–313–31336–9 (alk. paper)
    1. Young adult poetry, American—History and criticism.   2. Young adult
poetry—Themes, motives.   3. Young adults—Books and reading.   I. DeLong, Janice, 1943–
 PS309.Y69 S39 2002
809.1'0071'073—dc21   2001033719

British Library Cataloguing in Publication Data is available.

Library of Congress Catalog Card Number: 2001033719
ISBN: 0–313–31336–9

First published in 2002

Greenwood Press, 88 Post Road West, Westport, CT 06881
An imprint of Greenwood Publishing Group, Inc.
www.greenwood.com

Printed in the United States of America

∞

The paper used in this book complies with the
Permanent Paper Standard issued by the National
Information Standards Organization (Z39.48–1984).

10 9 8 7 6 5 4 3 2 1

Contents

Foreword

In a classroom in Cleveland, Paul writes:

> Poetry? All that mushy stuff?
> Who cares how many times she loves him,
> Or how many times she can count it?
> Who cares how many sonnets Shakespeare wrote,
> Or whether Milton was blind when he wrote his verses?
> Who needs to know iambic pentameter
> While walking by woods on a snowy evening?
> Who speaks in stanzas, talks in tetrameter?
> Not me. I got too many things to do.
> Nobody reads poetry; no one writes it.
> I'm serious. What's poetry gonna do for me?

I'm serious, too. Listen, Paul, poetry's going to help you figure out who you are and where you're heading. It's going to provide you with an emotional compass point from where you will gather strength to go down the road you choose.

Nobody reads poetry? Nobody writes it? Guess again.

I have been an English teacher for over thirty years and have seen first hand the verbal strivings of the human heart, the first attempts to give voice to what lies below the surface of supposedly happy teenage chatter.

Dora writes of her overprotective father, "I want to be a surgeon, Papa, and sever forever the ties that bind us." Marina worries about her boyfriend in Canada, "Will you still love me four hundred miles of telephone wire away?" Christina cries out in pain, "I give you everything, yet you love her," and DeShawn promises God, "I will never ask you for anything again if you let me make the team."

In city classroom, or on suburban street, from the northern plains, to the southern Delta, from small towns in Maine to large cities in California, students are wondering who they are and what they're going to be; these are the fundamental questions. Between the bravado and the silences, the socializing and the studying, the turbulent feelings and haunting questions still apply. It's a rite of passage.

And poetry supplies the answers, particularly this volume.

Young Adult Poetry is a treasure trove of answers. Good poetry, Paul, as reflected in these pages, can put us in touch with who we were, are, and will be. Students have it rough these days trying to figure out the pieces when they are the puzzle. Good poetry can provide the affirmation, "Hey, I am not alone; I've felt like that." It's the bright light of words that will illuminate the dark corners of the heart, the bright light of words that will enable teens to find a clear image of themselves.

Though many adults might feel that teenage emotion runs the gamut from A to A, those teachers, librarians, and parents who are involved with teens every day know that there is no crisis too small, no problem too big, that does not provoke a dramatic response. These educators will now have a brilliant new volume to help soften the edges of pain, lower the decibel of despair, and show their charges whatever the wound, whatever the triumph, there is somebody out there who has gained knowledge from the experience and has been willing to commit that experience to paper.

We are the sum of our poetic experiences, and we are no longer alone.

Nobody reads poetry? Nobody writes poetry? Are you kidding me, Paul?

Mel Glenn

Preface

Young Adult Poetry: A Survey and Theme Guide is designed to assist teachers, librarians, and parents in the most efficient and effective selection of poetry for use in the classroom or counseling setting. This volume is organized into four main divisions. Section one features individual annotations of each work with associated bibliographical information. Entries in this section are numbered from one to one hundred ninety-eight. Section two is a thematic guide to more than 6,000 poems. The numbers given at the end of the poem titles listed in the theme guide refer to the numbered bibliographic annotations. Section three is composed of an index of the writers or compilers of nearly two hundred anthologies. The final section, indexes of book titles, illustrators, and other significant items, completes the text.

Titles chosen for this anthology cover works by contemporary, classic, and ancient writers, with styles as varied as the number of authors. Some collections are created by a single writer, such as Ralph Fletcher's tribute to first love, *I Am Wings*. Others include a wide range of contributors, as in the classic *Sleeping on the Wing: An Anthology of Modern Poetry with Essays on Reading and Writing* edited by Kenneth Koch and Kate Farrell, which addresses such universal topics as life and death. Annotated entries for 198 poetry books span age levels from those traditionally considered to be for children through those exclusively for young adults and on to collections for adults. Persons interested in increasing the poetry holdings of their library or classroom will find this guide to be an invaluable collection development tool. The main component of this guide is the brief annotations arranged in alphabetical order by author, editor, compiler, or collector. Illustrators are listed after the title. Number of pages and recommended grade levels are also given. Annotations conclude with a listing of special helps such as indexes or biographical sketches that are supplied in the work.

Selections vary in length and breadth. Some are anthologies of many authors focusing on a single theme, such as Robert Hull's collection, *Breaking Free: An Anthology of Human Rights Poetry*. Others may cover a number of themes yet follow a chronology such as Lee Bennett Hopkins compilation, *Hand in Hand: An American History through Poetry*. Others may create an atmosphere so real that the reader feels transported to the location, as in David Harrison's *Wild Country: Outdoor Poems for Young People* or Mel Glenn's *Class Dismissed*. Some works focus on those verses that belong esoterically to the teen such as Lillian Morrison's verses on sports of all kinds in *Sprints and Distances* and Janet Wong's depictions of the beginning navigator, *Behind the Wheel: Poems about Driving*.

The other main section of this resource is the Thematic Guide to Poems. Since the thrust of this volume is toward the young adult reader, a broad range of topics is included in the theme guide. Educators, parents, and counselors who work with young adults know that on any given day the interest level of a teen may change from that of a child to that of an adult, sometimes almost within the hour—thus all poems listed (with corresponding themes) were selected with adolescents from twelve through eighteen in mind. Also, reading levels were considered, since skills vary widely from those of the struggling seventh or eighth grader to the gifted high school senior, and there must be verses readily accessible for all to enjoy. Themes and poems were chosen with both the curriculum goals of the teacher and interests of the students in mind. To meet these needs in both academic and recreational reading arenas, classroom teachers were surveyed, and nearly four hundred volumes of poetry were examined in preparation for this work. Other avenues of research included well-respected periodicals in the field of adolescent literature such as *The Horn Book Magazine* and *School Library Journal*. Textbooks such as *Literature for Today's Young Adult* by Alleen Pace Nilsen and Kenneth L. Donelson (Harper Collins College Publishers) and reference works such as *Best Books for Young Adult Readers* by Steven J. Calvert (R. R. Bowker) and *Books for You* published by the National Council of Teachers of English served as springboards for investigation.

Chief criteria for selection of volumes included in this reference guide were a variety of themes, ease of interpretation, creative use of language, interests of students, and usefulness in the classroom. Efforts were made to include those verses that would appeal to the rural as well as the suburban and urban reader. Recognizing that to say what will *appeal* to any population is taking a risk, however, an attempt was made to create a guide referencing volumes that will strike a spark of interest across the spectrum of adolescence. Samantha Abeel's creation, *Reach for the Moon*, was born out of her own struggle with a learning disability. While Donald Hall in *The Oxford Book of Children's Verse in America* reaches back to the 1640s for a serious look at life and also dips into the bizarre humor of Jack Prelutsky of the twentieth century. Mel Glenn offers food for thought in what it would be like to walk the tightrope of terror in *The Taking of Room 114: A Hostage Drama in Poems*, a topic as current as today's headlines. Included are five of Sara Holbrook's small, almost pocket-sized books, in which she gives readers a glimpse into the fragile world of junior high, where life is never the same two days in succession. Some single-subject volumes highlight one aspect of nature, such as Barbara Rogansky's *Winter Poems* or Martha Paulos' sometimes humorous, sometimes bizarre peek at a small, small world in *insectAsides*. Each selection was chosen for either the sheer enjoyment of the teen reader or for the teacher or librarian who is looking for a way to incorporate poetry across the curriculum—from literature and social studies to science and math. Hopefully, many of the verses will fill both criteria.

Although it is impossible to have a perfect balance of diversity in gender, ethnicity, religion, and those who survive disabilities, there is a breadth here that touches on all of these topics. Verses speaking from the heart of those who have lived with physical or mental handicaps are scattered throughout many anthologies, as are verses that address specific issues of faith. However, ethnicity was a bit easier to discover on an individual level. *Soul Looks Back in Wonder* by Tom Feelings, as well as a number of other selections speaks of the African American experience. *The Space Between Our Footsteps: Poems and Paintings from the Middle East* edited by Naomi Shihab Nye offers a tapestry of tastes both religious and cultural from an entire range of people. Janet S. Wong captures the feelings of two Asian based cultures, Korean and Chinese, in *A Suitcase of Seaweed and Other Poems*. Francis Lee, as an editor for the Smithsonian Institution, offers shining examples of teen writers in *When the Rain Sings: Poems by Young Native Americans*. Gary Soto provides insights into growing up Hispanic in *A Fire in My Hands*. Pat Mora, in *My Own True Name*, shares vignettes from her childhood of blended cultures. James Berry looks at his two cultures, Caribbean and British, from the inside of both in *Everywhere Faces Everywhere*.

Publication dates span more than fifty years, with the bulk of the selections being written in the 1990s. Most of the titles selected are currently in print, however, those that are not were found to be readily available on school or public library shelves. It is the belief of the compilers that books of quality that are available to teachers, librarians, and parents will be the ones that will be used, not just those that are new to the market. Some of the poems with the most profound messages are found in anthologies no longer in print.

The authors of this work have attempted to compile a reference guide that is easily accessible to all users. It is their desire to make poetry less intimidating to students and more inviting to the adults responsible for instruction in public, private, or home-school environments. With the variety listed here including old, new, humorous, tragic, rap, blues, rhyme, free verse, limerick, haiku, concrete, and other styles of verse, anyone who reads should find some lines that connect in a memorable way. The authors hope that teachers, librarians, or parents will no longer feel that they have to wait until there is time to "do a unit" on poetry to share with adolescents the creative experience that stems from this special form of literature. Perhaps, with the assistance of this anthology, poetry can become everyday fare.

Acknowledgments

We would like to express our appreciation to student assistants Amanda Creech, Wendy Rich, Melita Kendrick and Charity Laughlin for their cheerful service in compiling data for the Thematic Guide. To teachers Louanne Erdman, and Betsy Caballero, who shared ideas of favorite poets, and Kara DeLong, who researched, we give our thanks. To Shelli Warner, whose technology skills often rescued us from computer never-never land, we are greatly indebted.

To our husbands, Ron and Bob, for their continued understanding and encouragement, we express our deep gratitude.

The Guide: Annotated Bibliographical Entries

1 Abdul, Raoul, ed., *The Magic of Black Poetry*, illus. by Dane Burr, Dodd, Mead and Company, 1972 (hardcover), ISBN 0–396–06513–9, 118 pp., grades 6 and up.

A virtual smorgasbord of countries is represented by the poets selected to be included in Raoul Abdul's anthology. Pulling from countries such as Egypt, Guinea, Cuba, Nigeria, Brazil, Russia, and the United States, the compiler shows that black culture is international and finds expression in many languages. There is a mixture of titles by names well known to the poetry enthusiast, including Langston Hughes and Gwendolyn Brooks, selections by poets virtually unknown, and words from traditional spirituals and folk songs. Poems are selected specifically to be of interest to young readers, and most are one page or less in length. With thirteen subject divisions, the majority of readers should be able to find something to appeal to their palate. Starting with "Beginnings" and ending with "Tomorrows," other topics include "Springtime," "Love," "Nonsense," "Creatures," "Places," "Singing Words," "Ballads and Legends," "Christmas," "Heroes," "Like It Is," and "Night." Simple line drawings introduce each section. An epilogue, "For a Poet," written by Countee Cullen, draws the collection to a close. Helps for the reader include biographical notes about the author, about the editor, and about the artist.

2 Abeel, Samantha, *Reach for the Moon*, illus. by Charles R. Murphy, Pfeifer-Hamilton, 1993 (hardcover), ISBN 1–57025–013–8, unpaged, grades 9–adult.

Samantha Abeel chose to make her stumbling block a stepping stone. Struggles with a learning disability in mathematical concepts left her anxious and withdrawn by the time she reached seventh grade. Through the insight of her mother and the encouragement of her English teacher, Samantha discovered her talent to write. Using the illustrations of family friend and internationally known water colorist Charles R. Murphy, Samantha developed her gift. *Reach for the Moon* is the result.

In the inspiring introduction to this project of hope, Abeel encourages readers with learning disabilities to find their gift and polish it until it gives off light to others. Chronicling the youthful author's passage from a rather bleak beginning in seventh grade to a luminous ninth grade, these pages could be of lasting significance to the parent, teacher, or young person who reads this book. The collection includes both lyrical essays and amazing poetry. Verses reflect the writer's response to the artist's exquisite watercolor paintings, which complement the text on facing pages. Themes vary from Samantha's personal revelations in "Self Portrait" and "Wellspring" to nature poems such as "Sunrise," and "Drawing the Curtain of Night." Other topics range from Native American heritage in "If You Want to See" to casualties of the Vietnam conflict in "Leaves in the Fall."

Practical information assists parents and teachers in identifying and finding help for learning disabled children in the closing section, "Samantha's Journey." Readers may find the section "Searching for Help" especially useful with its list of symptomatic behaviors and addresses of organizations established to meet the needs of these special young people. As a recipient of the Margot Marek Award, this book is highly recommended for all libraries.

3 Adams, Joseph, ed., *The Poet's Domain*, vol. 7 in Footprints on the Sands of Time Series, Road Publishers, 1993 (paperback), ISBN 1–880016–11–7, 80 pp., grades 10 and up.

This volume is part of a series published for the purpose of encouraging contemporary poets of a particular region to showcase their work. Contributing to this collection are sixty-five writers from Delaware, Maryland, Virginia, and the District of Columbia. Biographical information accompanies the verses.

Engagement is the theme of this volume, and its contributors invite readers to come and participate in a shared experience. Margaret Edwards writes of the power of memories in "Reflectons." Olive Lanham speaks of the eternal importance of a shared second of time in "Destination." Sandra Ginn Scoville involves all the senses in her poem, "Flying."

Young adults will enjoy these verses because they beg for interaction. Relationships, reality, and response are connecting threads in the collection. For those readers who wish to submit original work, there is an invitation extended by the publishers on the back cover. There are no chapter divisions. Each writer's work stands alone with brief biographical information sharing the page.

4 Adoff, Arnold, *Chocolate Dreams*, illus. by Turi MacCombie, Lothrop, Lee and Shepard Books, 1989 (hardcover), ISBN 0–688–06823–5, 63 pp., grades 6 and up.

Persons in need of a belly laugh, a giggle, or just a smile can read and be satisfied with *Chocolate Dreams*. Adoff has given his imagination free reign to express his obsession with that dark, rich substance so many people crave. The student whose stomach is rumbling as the teacher drones on will appreciate "In This Last Class Before Lunch, I Close My Eyes." Those who are sure we have been visited by UFOs can agree with "I Believe In the Theory That Says We Were Visited Long Ago." For the chocoholic or the person who has the incredible ability to eat just one sweet, dark-brown morsel, there are selections here to please. MacCombie's full-color and brown and white illustrations are as tempting as the verse. A note to the reader introduces the collection, and short biographies of author and artist bring it to a close.

5   Adoff, Arnold, ed., *I Am the Darker Brother: An Anthology of Modern Poems by African Americans*, illus. by Benny Andrews, Simon and Schuster Books for Young Readers, 1997 (hardcover), ISBN 0–689–81241–8, 208 pp., grades 10 and up.

Published in 1968 as one of the first collections of poetry written by black writers, *I Am the Darker Brother* has made a major impact on the literary world. Still a classic after more than thirty years of being in print, this new edition is more than a simple reprint of the original. The addition of titles by twenty-one new poets, including ten women, has strengthened and broadened its offerings. As before, it gives expression to some of the most powerful voices of the African American experience. Verses by highly respected names such as Langston Hughes, James Weldon Johnson, Maya Angelou, Paul Laurence Dunbar, and Gwendolyn Brooks fill the pages with their poignant offerings. Although this collection has been published as a book for young readers, Adoff has chosen titles that do not avoid the difficult issues of racism and injustice. "The Lynching" and "So Quietly" expose the extreme horrors experienced by many. "Incident" and "We Wear the Mask" tell of the pain caused by more subtle expressions of prejudice. While "Montgomery: For Rosa Parks," and "Frederick Douglass" honor heroes who rose above their circumstances, "For My People" and "Listen Children" encourage pride of identity.

Extensive helps are given the reader through indexes to authors and to the first lines of poems. Author biographies fill fifteen pages, while nine pages are given to notes explaining the terms used in various poems. In some cases historical and biographical information expands the readers' understanding of the context of the work. Rudine Sims Bishop introduces the book with "Note From a Darker Sister" followed by Nikki Giovanni's foreword entitled "The Poem Speaks." The anthologist's own words conclude the collection in his afterword: "Thirty Years After Words."

6   Adoff, Arnold, *I Am the Running Girl*, illus. by Ronald Himler, Harper and Row, 1979 (hardcover), ISBN 0–06–020094–4, 36 pp., grades 6 and up.

Arnold Adoff steps inside the head of a young teenage runner to share with readers the motivation, the strategy, and the love of running that drive her in pursuit of her sport. Anyone who runs will identify with the pain, the hopes, the sheer exhilaration of speed expressed in verse. Black and white sketches by Ronald Himler enhance each double-page spread of this single poem volume.

7 Adoff, Arnold, *Love Letters*, illus. by Lisa Desimini, The Blue Sky Press, 1997 (hardcover), ISBN 0–590–48478–8, unpaged, grades 7 and up.

Arnold Adoff, already known to audiences of older adolescents, conspires with Lisa Desimini in this picture book to create a collage not only in illustration but of verse as well. The choice of a dove bearing a love letter adorns the front cover and lends an air of commitment and admission of affection usually reserved for the relationships of older teens. However, the verses within the work include those from secret admirers and responses from those who would be just as happy if unadmired—characteristic of the entire range of adolescent responses to the first flutters of love.

Desimini's choice of collage is reminiscent of the old-fashioned homemade valentine. She uses items common to the classroom, home, and yard or garden. For example, there are photographs of a teacher working at her desk to whom two letters are addressed. In one she is Mrs. Nicely, in the other she is Miss McNasty. There is also an allusion to the change in tone reflected in the illustrations given on adjacent pages. Items as common as blackboard and chalk, snow and sticks, and buttons and fabric are used to create a wide variety of moods. For the poems set at home, Desmini affectionately symbolizes Dad as Mr. Potato Head in his couch potato role and Mom as a jigsaw puzzle—reflecting the speaker, not the parent.

Adoff captures the innocence of worship-from-afar in "Dear Ms. Back Row" and "Dear New Boy." He poignantly reveals unrequited love in "Dear Playground Snow Girl" and the sassy response, "Dear Playground Snow Boy." Yet, even in these, the reader has no feeling of permanent rejection—it is a temporary loss that may be changed by tomorrow. The clumsiness of bodies growing too rapidly for grace is expressed in "Dear Tall Girl at Front Table," and the fickleness of first love in "Dear Fill-in-Your-Own-Name" (A hint for this one, his father owns a really neat new copy machine.) There are even love letters for mom, dad, and grandma to round out this refreshing collection. For the collector of this award-winning poet's works, this will be one of the volumes to which the reader will return again and again, especially when some inspiration is needed on February 14.

8 Adoff, Arnold, ed., *My Black Me: A Beginning Book of Black Poetry*, E.P. Dutton, 1974 (hardcover), ISBN 0–52545216–8 83 pp., grades 6 and up.

Adoff has compiled a collection of fifty poems that center on African American cultural heritage. Divided into six untitled sections, their emphasis varies.

Respect for the black race and pride of identity are found in "My People" and "Listen Children." Frustrations resulting from cross-cultural relations find voice in from "Riot Rimes U.S.A. #79" and "It Aint No." The strength of family reigns in "Portrait," and African American heroes take their place of honor in titles like "Ali" and "Death of Dr. King #1." This volume contains a six-page section of biographical information on the twenty-five participating poets. It tells where they were born, what they have written, and what they are doing now. In addition to the table of contents, there is an index to authors and an index to first lines.

9 Adoff, Arnold, *Slow Dance: Heart Break Blues*, illus. by William Cotton, Lothrop, Lee and Shepard Books, 1995 (hardcover), ISBN 0–688–10569–6, 88 pp., grades 7 and up.

The black and white photo collages of William Cotton act as effective dividers to the untitled sections of Adoff's poems of adolescent life. The excitement and anguish of teenage love presented in "This Hug, This Kiss, This Hand," insecurities about physical appearances in "Listen to the Voice In Your Head," and problematic family relationships presented in "You Never Really Listen," are subjects of major importance to the young person. The dangers and temptations of drug use receive attention in six titles including "Chemistry Lesson after Class," and "Just Say No." School sports and concerns about the condition of our world round out the topics presented. Though some titles like "Here in Our City" express concerns particular to urban youth, most are universal in their appeal. A short biographical sketch of the author is found at the back of the book. Adoff's words tumble out on these pages to create images instantly recognizable to the adolescent. There is no obscurity here, but straightforward expression of feelings that any young person can understand. From six words to a full page in length, no two poems are presented the same way on the page but are arranged in patterns to strengthen the message of the verse. No matter which subject is being pursued in the individual poems, one overall theme permeates the book. The author expresses the adolescent need to know if the love they give will be returned.

10 Adoff, Arnold, *Sports Pages*, illus. by Steve Kuzma, J.B. Lippincott, 1986 (hardcover), ISBN 0–397–32102–3, 79 pp., grades 7 and up.

"Action" would be the best single descriptor for this collection of thirty-seven poems, written to resonate with the heartbeat of many adolescents. Adoff, who is well known for his many contributions to the field of children's and young adult literature, has focused his rhythms of motion and meter to speak to both sides of the brain. The author takes the readers to the field, track, and the gym and captures the sacrifice and success, victory and loss. "Now: In This Frozen Moment on This Moving World Through Space" will call up memories of soccer-stars-to-be who sometimes question why they do what they do, just to play. "Afternoons: One" addresses the angst of a football player who glances at the sidelines just in time to see the coach turn his back on a less than successful play. "Sweet" depicts the indescribable rush of watching the basketball swish through the hoop. "Even the Light Seems Dark" will speak to those who have to put in extra time lifting weights to regain what has been lost as the result of an injury. "Ground Bound" swings with the rhythm of the gymnast working out on the parallel bars. "Equal Curses on Two Long Lines of Equally Short Ancestors" expresses the frustration of one who, because of his height deficiency expresses his dark thoughts for both the opposing pitcher, and those who bequeathed him his stature. Other sports such as horse racing, skating, wrestling, tennis and more are addressed. The concluding piece reveals why sports exist and hold such fierce attraction for the young. It is entitled "We Have Our Moments."

Uses for this volume are as myriad as they are obvious. For the undeveloped literary mind, for those who love both sports and the arts, for those who have not yet found where they excel but enjoy the vicarious thrill, this collection should hold great appeal. Reading, writing, collecting, and illustrating all have boundless possibilities with Adoff's great idea as a foundation.

11   Agard, John, comp., *Life Doesn't Frighten Me at All*, Henry Holt and Co., 1989 (hardcover), ISBN: 0–8050–1237–0, 96 pp., grades 9 and up.

Agard has collected poems from around the world to appeal to the palate of the teenager. In his introduction Agard asserts his determination to convince the reader that poetry is indeed something attuned to rather than removed from everyday life. Choosing the works of male and female poets, both young and old, Agard's selections take the reader on a tour of the world from Bangladesh to Denmark. Some of the writers included are well known for their work while others are still schoolchildren. Small personal notes at the end of many of the poems afford the reader insight into the background of the writer and the verse. Two pages of "Poetry Patter" at the back of the book contain twelve of the poets' comments on life and on poetry. Following these pages is an index of poets and an index of first lines. With topics inspired by problems as diverse as wanting a "Spell to Banish a Pimple," coping with the fallout from "Divorce," or understanding the difficulties of cross-cultural relations in "If My Right Hand," this volume demonstrates amply the compiler's view that there is something for everyone in poetry. Combining all of these elements, Agard makes a strong argument to convince teens that they do not need to fear poetry, but can enjoy reading it. Going a step further, they can use it to express their feelings on any topic, from the serious to the mundane.

12 Angelou, Maya, *The Complete Collected Poems of Maya Angelou*, Random House, 1994 (hardcover), ISBN 0–697–42895–X, 273 pp., grades 11 and up.

Known for her autobiographical works, theater productions, and appointments of note by Presidents Ford and Carter, as well as her office with the Southern Christian Leadership Conference and numerous literary awards, Maya Angelou has an established reputation in American culture. Long the champion of blacks and women, she focuses much of her writing on their plight.

Four poetry anthologies are brought together to form *The Complete Collected Poems*. Each chapter in the work represents one of her previous books. To read the titles is to gain some idea of the range of themes included—"Just Give Me a Cool Drink of Water 'fore I Die," "Oh Pray My Wings Are Gonna Fit Me Well," "And Still I Rise," and "I Shall Not Be Moved." The final chapter consists of "On the Pulse of Morning," which was read by Ms. Angelou at the inauguration of President William Clinton. In the collection are threads of love lost in "Poor Girl," loneliness in "The Traveler," many on observations of life, as in "Alone," and a wide range of poems taken from the stages of life, as in "Life Doesn't Frighten Me" and "On Aging."

Teachers, librarians, and parents will find this anthology of value in seeking out verses that passionately mirror the black experience. The sensitive reader will feel pain in the author's poems on slavery. Sex, drugs, lost love, and social injustice are predominant themes in the bulk of her work. There are also selections with glorious descriptions of Africa (Ms. Angelou's home for a time), of a mother's love and acceptance, and of faith. All are powerful and would generate thoughtful discussion among young adults.

13 Anglund, Joan Walsh, *Memories of the Heart*, illus. by Joan Walsh Anglund, Random House, 1984 (hardcover), ISBN 0–394–5376–6, 63 pp., grades 6 and up.

For the educator searching for inspirational quotes for bulletin boards, this tiny volume is a gold mine. Self-control, forgiveness, friendship, and unselfish love all are major themes found in these simple meditations. From three lines to twenty-three, most selections are an ideal length for posting in the classroom. No index is given to these twenty-eight poems, but none is needed. The volume is illustrated by the author's signature pen and ink drawings.

14 Asch, Frank, *Cactus Poems*, illus. by Ted Levin, Harcourt, Brace and Company, 1998 (hardcover), ISBN 0–15–200676–1, 48 pp., grades 8 and up.

Asch and Levin explore the energy and vitality of all forms of life populating four North American deserts in this single-theme book. The poet and photographer are both residents of New England, yet guide readers through the Chihuahuan Desert, the Great Basin, the Mojave Desert, and the Sonoran Desert and manage to combine the awe of tourists with the insight of naturalists. Levin's astonishing photographs of scenes, both panoramic and minute, are sufficiently poetic to stir the emotions without a word being read. Asch's accompanying text reaches out to the audience with such authenticity that cottontails, coyotes, and rocks seem to be speaking. Such a balance raises the question of whether this is an illustrated poetry book or a picture book with accompanying verses. A special feature of this work is an informative section entitled "Some Notes on Desert Life." In this helpful guide, Asch gives a wealth of knowledge succinctly condensed into single paragraphs focusing on the theme of each poem. Levin adds the location and date of corresponding photographs. The range of topics covered in this thin volume is as vast as the land itself. Readers may gaze at the brilliant shades of orange and blue splashing the sand dunes of Stovepipe Wells as they enjoy "Break Free." In contrast, there is a protective emotion aroused by the hushed "voice" of the diminutive mother in "Hummingbird Song." For variety in form, there is "Saguaro," written in concrete style to emphasize the value of each part of the stalwart cactus, and the jumpy lines of "Cottontail," who is valiantly eluding his natural enemies. The breathtaking beauty of sunset at Signal Hill, Arizona, with the affectionate farewell, "If the Earth Were Small," is an appropriate tribute to this mysterious, fascinating, and sometimes deadly section of the country.

15 Baber, Bob Henry, George Ella Lyon, and Gurney Norman, eds., *Old Wounds, New Words: Poems from the Appalachian Poetry Project*, Jesse Stuart Foundation, 1994 (hardcover), ISBN: 0–945084–44–7, 203 pp., grades 7 and up.

This collection was initiated in 1979 by a grant from the Witter Bymer Foundation. In order to encourage would be poets, the editors held nineteen poetry workshops in various locations in six states. Combining the poetry created in these workshops with works found in magazines and journals, the editors gathered poems by ninety-one southern Appalachian poets. An extensive introduction provides a history of the development of Appalachian poetry and an explanation of the importance of this form of communication in a culture that has traditionally expressed itself in story and song. Short personal profiles of each poet are included in a special section at the back of the book. Poems are presented in order by author names. A few major themes of particular importance to the Appalachian area dominate this anthology. Sadness, confusion, and a sense of helplessness caused by modern exploitation of the land are expressed intensely in "The Last Unmined Vein." A reevaluation of the past with a reclaiming of its positive aspects is the subject of "Ebbing and Flowing Spring." The tension created between the pull of the old against the new is found in

"Old-Timer to Grandchild." Overriding these concerns is a feeling of kinship with the earth as shown in "Climbing the Linville Falls." Though strongly regional, the poems touch on universal concerns that young people may face, such as the frustration experienced by a powerlessness to stop change, the uncertainty brought on by a need to reidentify oneself in the face of change, and anger at the stereotypes often placed on groups of people by society. *Old Wounds, New Worlds* presents the normal stages of life with an Appalachian twist.

16 Begay, Shonto, *Navajo: Visions and Voices Across the Mesa*, Scholastic, 1995 (hardcover), ISBN 0–590–46153–2, 48 pp., grades 7 and up.

Using his talent as a painter and a poet, Shonto Begay combines stories of ancient times with reflections on his own life as a Navajo Indian. The overriding theme echoes the continual struggle in his heart and mind to reach a balance between the centuries-old culture of his people and the pull of contemporary society. In the perspectives of both cultures, he emphasizes the responsibility of all people to love and protect the earth. In "Echoes" the author begins his anthology by sharing with the reader the spiritual elements of his background. Memories of childhood follow in poems such as "Grandmother" and "Darkness at Noon." Members of his community and community life are introduced through "Second Night' and "Down Highway 163." The selections close with hope for the future conveyed through "Into the New World" and "Early Spring."

The quality of Begay's artwork is attested to by the fact that many of his paintings form a permanent part of museum collections. His technique of using small repetitive brush strokes produces works of great power and strength. The volume includes a valuable introduction by the author, a table of contents to access the poems, and an index to the individual paintings. The pictures and the verse together make an excellent resource for teachers wishing to tie together the fields of science, history, and literature.

17 Berry, James, ed., *Classic Poems to Read Aloud*, illus., James Mayhew, Larousse Kingfisher Chambers, 1995 (hardcover), ISBN 1–85697–987–3, 256 pp., grades 7 and up.

"Classic" is no mere adjective in the title of this collection. As James Berry discloses in the introduction, he sought out those poems immediately identified as time tested as well as those with the potential to be enjoyed by posterity. English voices from locations as diverse as Native American hunting grounds, Ireland, and Africa are among those represented.

Eleven chapters with titles as intriguing as the poetry provide structure for this anthology. "Varied Bodies, Varied Means" houses "The Donkey" by G.K. Chesterton and "Bats" by Randall Jarrell as well as other expressions of both man and beast. "Journeys of Summer, Fall, and People," evokes responses to the seasons with works such as "Ode to Autumn" by John Keats and "Nature" by H.D. Carberry painting pictures of seasons in vastly different climates. "Water, Wild Wind and Fire" shelters responses to forces of nature with "Until I Saw the Sea" by Lillian Moore, "Wind" by Ted Hughes, "Weathers" by Thomas Hardy, and others. "Magic and Mysteries" reveals works as varied as "Spells" by James Reeves and Lewis Carroll's "Jabberwocky." "Lighthearted Happenings" contains verses ranging from "Prayer to Laughter" by John Agard to "Elegy on the Death of a Mad Dog" by Oliver Goldsmith. The list of familiar and those not so well known goes on. More frequently considered classics such as "The Rime of the Ancient Mariner" (Samuel Taylor Coleridge), "O, My Luve's Like a Red, Red Rose" (Robert Burns), Sonnets 18 and 29 by William Shakespeare, "The Lady of Shalott" and "Charge of the Light Brigade" by Alfred Lord Tennyson are also found between the covers of this versatile volume. If one were restricted to a single anthology to share with young adults, this may very well be it. Useful features include an index of titles and first lines as well as an index of poets.

18 Berry, James, *Everywhere Faces Everywhere*, illus. Reynold Ruffins, Simon and Schuster, 1996 (hardcover), ISBN: 0–689–80996–4, 80 pp., grades 8 and up.

Slim though the volume may be, it speaks clearly about the faces of people everywhere. Use of dialect and colloquial expressions gives this book a cosmopolitan air while maintaining its rural charm. In the introduction, Berry states that it is his desire to reveal reflections from his own childhood in the Caribbean and his adult life in the United Kingdom. He successfully shares experiences across cultures through language unique to each group of people while acknowledging that children and young adults have their own culture, no matter what the geographical location, skin color, or climate.

Beginning with "Bits of Early Days," Berry paints word pictures of impressions remembered from childhood. The next section, entitled "Look, No Hands," focuses on various aspects of nature. In its earthy intimacy, "Trap of a Clash" is the collection that reminds the reader of a walk around a Caribbean village. "Watching a Dancer" contains the title poem and others that are reminiscent of an affectionate observer sharing thoughts with a younger companion. Finally, "Fish and Water Woman" reveals both the mystical and emotional dimension of island life. Forms of poetry contained in this little book range from haiku to rap, so there is something to appeal to almost any reader.

19 Berry, James, *When I Dance: Poems*, Harcourt Brace Jovanovich, 1998 (hardcover), ISBN 0–15–295568–2, 120 pp., grades 9 and up.

Just as poetry has been said to sing, James Berry has taught it to dance. From Caribbean sunlit shores and London's open air markets, Berry leads readers with rollicking rhythms and soul-sad blues through two distinct cultures. Choosing to speak from the perspective of the ever-changing young adult heart, Berry addresses universal themes ranging from joy to isolation. His style moves from didactic proverbs through chants and riddles on to rap. An invaluable introduction sets the stage for the following seven chapters. Further explanatory material is supplied in Berry's "Notes on the Poems" page. These verses are designed for a variety of responses. The teacher or group leader should be prepared for accompanying hand claps with some, such as "Nativity Play Plan," or finger snaps with others, such as "Let Me Rap You My Orbital Map." "Jamaican Caribbean Proverbs" may pose a challenge to read aloud, as it is written in the native tongue, but Berry has included the English translation. Taken altogether, this sparkling collection makes the connection between rhythm and verse that may very well create new fans for poetry as teens recognize its affinity with dance.

20   Berry, Wendell, *Entries*, Pantheon Books, 1994 (hardcover), ISBN 0–679–42609–4, 88 pp., grades 9 and up.

In *Entries* author Wendell Berry shows great respect for family and for rural living through poems that dignify the simple life. An extension of these thoughts is shown in the care and regard for the environment that is demonstrated in his titles "The Reassurer" and "The Storm." In contrast, Berry sees much foolishness in modern society, an opinion highlighted in his poem "Madness." The quality of character exhibited in a person's life also appears to be of great importance to the author. In his poems "Even in Darkness" and "Duality" he stresses the importance of love. In "Enemies" and "To My Mother" forgiveness plays an important role. Though touting an unsophisticated lifestyle, Berry's poems are far from simplistic. They are contemplative and classical in scope while retaining a devotion to farm, home, and the community of mankind. Although not written specifically for young adults, these selections will convey to young people wisdom and an encouragement to live well.

21   Bolin, Frances Schoonmaker, ed., *Poetry for Young People: Emily Dickinson*, illus. by Chi Chung, Sterling Publications, 1994 (hardcover), ISBN 0–80690–635–9, 48 pp, grades 6–9.

Frances Bolin, in collaboration with Chi Chung, has created a charming collection of poems by Emily Dickinson. This shy poet, who spent much of her life within the confines of her garden, her home, or her room, displays great insight into life and gives the reader much to ponder in poems such as "In This Short Life" and "I Dwell in Possibility." The lines found in "There Is No Frigate Like a Book" and "The Moon Was But a Chin of Gold" stir the imagination to dream of far off places. Simple delight in ordinary things are fostered by "A

Bird Came Down the Walk" and "A Soft Sea Washed Around the House." The mystery of death is spoken of in "I Have Not Told My Garden Yet."

Choosing from Miss Dickinson's more than 1,700 poems, Bolin has brought together a selection that should encourage adolescents to look at the world with a sense of wonder. Some of Chi Chung's illustrations may seem a little young for the older adolescent, but they are an effective complement to the simplicity of Dickinson's poetry. Understanding of the poet is expanded with a biographical introduction. Definitions of difficult words are given at the bottom of each page of poetry. An index is included to provide alphabetical access to the titles.

22   Burleigh, Robert, *Hoops*, illus. by Stephen T. Johnson, Harcourt, Brace and Company, NY, 1997 (hardcover), ISBN 0–15–201450–0, unpaged, grades 6 and up.

This single poem title places the reader in the middle of a game of basketball. With few words Burleigh conveys to the reader the feel of the ball and the excitement of the game. The fluid motion of the players, the beauty of the body movement, and the challenge of competition make the reader an integral part of the action. The vocabulary and the soft, yet vivid illustrations make this a picture book for teens and adults instead of for children. Though the flow of language and the beauty of the illustrations can be appreciated by all, those who play and love the game will understand this work the best.

23   Carlson, Lori M., ed., *Cool Salsa: Bilingual Poems on Growing Up Latino in the United States*, Henry Holt and Company, 1994 (hardcover), ISBN 0–8050–3135–9, 136 pp., grades 8 and up.

Thirty-six contemporary Latino poets effectively express the Spanish American experience in America in these energetic works. Their verses bring together many strands to weave a colorful tapestry of Hispanic life in America. Through the words of these storytellers in verse, the reader can see, hear, and taste the Latino culture. Divided by broad subject areas such as "School Days," "Home and Homeland," "Memories," "Hard Times," "Time to Party," and "A Promising Future," they reveal the joy as well as the pain of being torn between two cultures. Many poems included appear in both Spanish and in translation. Some are a true bilingual mix of both languages.

The poets of *Cool Salsa* speak to private issues of home and family in poems such as "Memories of Uncle Pety." Public issues, such as revolution, are addressed in "My Memories of the Nicaraguan Revolution." The search for public acceptance is expressed in "America, It's Hard to Get Your Attention." Above all, many, such as "The Calling," voice a positive hope for the future. If there is one underlying theme it may be the search for identity or the need to adjust to new ways without losing an appreciation for the old. Many express the frustration of needing to be absorbed into the general culture of the United States without losing their own personal selfhood. Besides being a means of expression for the Latino young adult, this search for self-definition in spite of difficult circumstances is where *Cool Salsa* speaks best to all teens. Helpful introductions by the compiler and by one of the featured poets explain the impetus behind creating the collection. There is a very useful glossary of Spanish terms arranged under individual poem titles. Short biographical notes about each poet close out the valuable collection.

24   Carroll, Joyce Armstrong, and Edward E. Wilson, comps., *Poetry after Lunch: Poems to Read Aloud*, Absey and Company, 1997 (paperback), ISBN 1–888842–03–2, 163 pp., grades 8 and up.

If the title is not inviting enough to make teachers and parents of teens want to sample the wares in this collection, the distinction of being the recipient of two awards may do so. Winner of the New York Public Library Books for the Teen Age award, 1998, and an ALA winner of Best Books for Young Adults for the same year, this anthology has much to offer the caring adult who desires to create a love of poetry in the heart of young adults. Carroll and Wilson make the work appealing right from the table of contents with clock face motifs decorating the title of each meal-related chapter title. Their introduction invites the reader to bite right in and expect a full course with beverages and desserts. The appetizer for readers is that Carroll and Wilson share the eager question their students have posed, "Aren't you going to read some poetry today?"

The sixty-four contributors are contemporary—from Archibald Macleish in the early decades of the 1900s to Gary Soto in 1995. Topics cover cultures eclectically from George Ella Lyons in the Appalachians to Diana Chang, who is both Chinese and American. Emotions touched by the pieces run the full gamut. "Ode to My Southern Drawl" by Kathi Appelt asserts the security of being comfortable with one's own language and accompanying identity. In contrasting mood, Nancy Willard deposits the reader in the seat of anguish as an expectant mother careens toward the hospital with an at-risk baby who won't wait for delivery in "For You, Who Didn't Know." For another change of pace, David Wagoner poses the final word in six "Epitaphs," brimming with word play and humor. The breadth of this collection is certain to appeal to many young adults, and the power of many selections will spark stimulating discussions or simply inspire greater love of the genre. Accompanying the introduction, other special aids are the acknowledgments page and indexes to poem titles and poets.

25   Carson, Jo, *Stories I Ain't Told Nobody Yet: Selections from the People Pieces,* Orchard Books, 1989 (hardcover), ISBN 0–531–05808–5, 83 pp., grades 8 and up.

Many of the subjects dealt with in this collection are adult situations, such as loss of a job, domestic violence, and fears for the destruction of the land. To the young adult growing up in families touched by these issues, however, the scenes will be all too familiar. Certainly young persons who call Appalachia home can identify with the anger expressed against cultural prejudice in "Mountain People." The conflict between generations seen in "My Daughter Got Divorced," and "I've Worked This Place," ring true in any setting. But all the verse is not dismal. There is humor in "I Spent the First Years of My Life" and "Now, George Is Sick," and a refreshing, down-to-earth quality permeates the collection. Created from stories overheard from other's conversations, the forty-nine poems were adapted to use as monologues or dialogues in public performance. Written in dialect, they are organized into five sections titled "Neighbors and Kin," "Observations," "Relationships," "Work," and "We Say of Ourselves." Some of the selections may be useful to students in fulfilling assignments for speech or drama.

26   Carter, Jimmy, *Always a Reckoning and Other Poems,* illus. by Sarah Elizabeth Chuldenko, Times Books, 1995 (hardcover), ISBN 0–8129–2434–7, 130 pp., grades 9 and up.

Classified as vanity publishing, Jimmy Carter's anthology of verse is nevertheless worthy of a thoughtful read. Like the poet, these titles can be described as unpretentious and quietly intelligent. Separated into four groups, the forty-four poems discuss "People," "Places," "Politics," and "Private Lives." Many, such as "Rachel," describe the people and events that shaped the author's early life. "Why We Get Cheaper Tires from Liberia" and "Progress Does Not Always Come Easy" touch upon his political and social convictions. "Reflection of Beauty in Washington" is a marveling at the beauty of nature. For students of history and English, exposure to this volume provides a worthwhile glimpse into the soul of one of the nation's contemporary presidents. Poems are listed in a table of contents, an index of titles, and an index of first lines. The president's granddaughter, Sarah Elizabeth Chuldenko, has provided black and white sketches to accompany each verse.

27   Clark, Stephen R., *The Godtouch,* Northwoods Press, 1985 (paperback), ISBN 0–89002–242–9, 63 pp., grades 8 and up.

Powerful imagery fills the pages of *The Godtouch* written by Stephen R. Clark. In this slim volume, the author conveys with dramatic word pictures his responses to the physical, emotional, and spiritual experiences of his life. Whether writing of love in "Thumbs and Pulses," sunburns in "Seasonal Hell," or intense spiritual experiences in "Moment of Always Meeting," Clark displays sensitivity without sentimentality. Humor also surfaces in selections like "Prayer at Midwinter," a title that is sure to be enjoyed by those who have lived in chilly northern climates. Divided into six sections, the offerings cover love, nature, Christmas, Easter, the need for life changes, man's search for God, and changes in relationships.

A table of contents provides access to poem titles, and a biographical note at the back of the book introduces the author. Young adults should respond well to the poignant emotional content and the vividly descriptive language.

28   Cole, William, ed., *Fireside Book of Humorous Poetry*, original illustrations by John Tenniel and others, Simon and Schuster, 1959 (hardcover), ISBN 0–671–25850–8, 522 pp., grades 8 and up.

William Cole, already known to poetry lovers for his own talent, has collected more than five hundred pages of light-hearted verse from both sides of the Atlantic in this comprehensive volume. Selections are drawn from a wide range of contributors, including those who are best known for their amusing verses as well as others who would be first recognized as writers of more serious works. The collection is divided into nineteen chapters with intriguing titles ranging from "Eccentrics and Individualists" and "Edibles, Potables, and Smokeables" to "Playful and Tricky" and "Harangue and Misanthropy." Length of individual entries varies from those with as few as four lines to narratives of several pages—each containing humor of one type or another. Puns, parody, slapstick, and subtle innuendo are all represented, and there is indeed something to make everyone smile. As would be expected, there is a generous helping of Ogden Nash. "Tableau at Twilight" shares a touching scene of a small child with an ice cream cone spending memorable moments at the close of day with a fastidious parent. W.S. Gilbert adds a touch of the dark, meditative wit of one waiting for execution in "To Sit in Solemn Silence." This volume is well named, as it would serve nicely for an entire family to enjoy in front of a cozy fire, with each sharing his/her favorite compositions. This work draws on those old favorites from childhood while also introducing young adults to writers on more adult themes with a touch more sophistication. As always is true with a volume of this magnitude, only a fraction of the poems included are listed among the themes in this work. Once introduced to Cole's collection, each reader will find those verses that appeal to his own sense of humor—a rewarding way to ensnare the reluctant reader.

29 De la Mare, Walter, ed., *Come Hither: A Family Treasury of Best-Loved Rhymes and Poems for Children*, Avenel Books, 1990 (hardcover), ISBN 0–517–02743–7, 799 pp., grades 7 and up.

In 1957, when this anthology was initially published, there was little, if any, distinction made between children's and young adult literature. Thus, the designation of "Children" in the title may deter some contemporary parents, teachers, or adolescents who would otherwise sample its verses. The revered editor draws work from more than 150 masters such as Shakespeare, Frost, Poe, Whitman, and others of their stature. Not all of the more than five hundred pieces will appeal to the twenty-first-century adolescent, but a number will. De la Mare introduces the work with a lengthy author's note explaining his inspiration for the collection. Sixteen chapters follow with such timeless titles as "Dance, Music and Bells"; "War"; "Old Tales and Balladry"; and "Evening and Dream." Concluding resources list an index of authors, index of poems, and an index of notes.

30 Dillard, Annie, ed., *Mornings Like This*, Harper Collins, 1995 (hardcover), ISBN 0–06–017155–3, 75 pp., grades 10 and up.

This collection of found poems was not expressly compiled for young adults, nor does it fit the format usually expected from the genre. However, there are thought-provoking works that the teenager will enjoy. Annie Dillard has assembled bits and pieces of text from writings dating back to 1828 through the 1990s. Selections cover topics from science to the arts. A number are translations. David Grayson wrote the title poem to extol the glories of the day for *The Countryman's Year* that was published in 1936. David W. McKay and Bruce G. Smith's contribution, "Getting Started," was discovered in *Space and Science Projects for Young Scientists* (1986) and states some cautions regarding gravity and falling bodies. S.K. Heninger offers insightful observations on thunder and lightning from his *Handbook of Renaissance Meteorology* under Dillard's subtitle, "A View of Certain Wonderful Effects." "Junior High School English" by Briggs, McKinney, and Skeffington gives the contemporary reader a view of the challenges to middle schoolers in 1926. The strength of this collection lies in broadening the reader's concept of poetry. It may also serve as an inspiration to look for found poems. The author's note following the table of contents provides an explanation for the theme of the collection.

31 Downie, Mary Alice, and Barbara Robertson, comps., *The New Wind Has Wings: Poems from Canada*, illus. by Elizabeth Cleaver, Oxford University Press, 1984 (hardcover), ISBN 0–19–540431–9, 110 pp., grades 7 and up.

First published in 1968, this updated version of Canadian verse includes delightful additions. In the original edition, brilliant collage, as well as and black and white linocuts established Elizabeth Cleaver as a children's book artist. Additional verses and illustrations embellish the current volume. More than eighty poems by fifty-six authors are included with Cleaver's expressive art gracing almost all of the pages. Some entries are succinct and thought provoking such as A.M. Klein's "Orders," which gives rather direct instructions to leave the reader alone with her thoughts. Other selections are narratives, such as Frank Davey's poignant verse "The Piano," which comments on what it is like to be a shy child who is instructed to play for visitors who have not the courtesy to listen. Some rejoice in the beauty of nature, as James Reaney's "June." Others record the fury of natural forces as Charles Sangster's "The Rapid." Although nature is a pervading topic, unique voices add freshness to the age-old theme. Special features include an index of poets and an acknowledgments page.

32 Duffy, Carol Ann, ed., *Stopping for Death: Poems of Death and Loss*, illus. by Trisha Rafferty, Henry Holt and Company, 1996 (hardcover), ISBN: 0–8050–4717–4, 144 pp., grades 10 and up.

This compilation of poems considers the subjects of death, mourning, and loss, which are universal to us all. Beginning with Emily Dickinson's "Because I Could Not Stop for Death" and ending with her own "And Then What," Duffy has collected eighty titles from around the world with a broad range of tone and varied levels of difficulty. Whether death is attributed to war as in "Killed in Action," suicide as in "The Suicides," or accident as in "Dead Dog," contributors explore feelings of grief and loss with courage and insight. Many touch on issues beyond death, such as the rejection felt in "Tich Miller" and the sorrow of injustice seen in "Come from That Window Child." Poems are arranged in alphabetical order by author's names. Also provided are a table of contents and an index of first lines. Whimsical pen and ink illustrations are scattered throughout.

33 Dunning, Stephen, Edward Lueders, and Hugh Smith, comps., *Reflections on a Gift of Watermelon Pickle . . . and Other Modern Verse*, Lee and Shepard Company, 1967, (ISBN 0–673–03363–5), 139 pp., grades 6 and up.

Since its publication, *Reflections on a Gift of Watermelon Pickle* has been a standard poetry text in high school classrooms. With the stated purpose of encouraging young people to read and enjoy literature, the editors carefully chose titles that would appeal to the adolescent. To accomplish this end, the compilers found works that cover a wide gamut of subject material from the ridiculous to the sublime, from the silly to the deadly serious. The humor of "Why Nobody Pets the Lion at the Zoo," for example, contrasts sharply with the ironic twist of "Earth." The optimistic tone of "Wonder Wander" differs greatly from the suicidal thoughts of "Too Blue." Selections like "Swift Things Are Beautiful," express an appreciation for the world around us while "The Forcast" and other titles probe the failings of society.

New poets are a part of the collection along with well-known names like Eve Merriam, Theodore Roetke, Elizabeth Coatsworth, and Dorothy Parker, but all selections speak in a straightforward manner without obscurity or classical references that might inhibit understanding. Though roughly grouped by subject matter that relates to nature, modern society, animals, family, personal success or failure, and ecology, the collection has no designated chapter divisions. A table of contents, however, and an author-title index aid in finding desired titles. Photos used as illustrations are artistically chosen and strengthen the emotional impact of the verse. Arranged effectively on the pages by designer Donald Marvine, all elements combine to create a timeless treasure with an appeal to a wide audience.

34   Dunning, Stephen, Edward Lueders, and Hugh Smith, comps., *Some Haystacks Don't Even Have Any Needle and Other Modern Poems*, Lothrop, Lee and Shepard, 1969 (hardcover), ISBN 0–8050–3668–7, 192 pp., grades 10 and up.

Compiled by the same editors as *Reflections On a Gift of Watermelon Pickle*, this volume presumably was created for the same purpose of gathering together in one place a selection of contemporary poetry that would appeal to the young adult reader. Its design and selection of verse, however, is more sophisticated in tone than its predecessor. A larger percentage of the verses included appeal to the older, thoughtful student. In place of photographs, reprints of works by well-known artists such as Paul Klee, and Edward Hopper are scattered throughout. All poems use contemporary language and images familiar to the teenage reader. Poems are grouped into seventeen sections, with no particular subject designation noted. There is an index of authors, an index of titles and an extensive acknowledgments section. Picture credits are listed at the front in alphabetical order by artist.

35   Eady, Cornelius, *You Don't Miss Your Water*, Henry Holt and Company, 1995 (hardcover), ISBN 0–8050–3667–9, 33 pp., grades 10 and up.

Reading through the twenty-one poems of this small anthology, the reader walks with the poet as he experiences the demise of his father's health and finally his death. Looking back on childhood experiences with this parent, the memories of parental rejection as experienced in "A Little Bit of Soap" and the grind of poverty in "Motherless Children" will resonate with young people living in that scene today. "I Ain't Got No Home" may awaken understanding of the fears that accompany those who are aging. Although the poet deals with the difficult issues of abusive relationships and death, his work manages to covey hope. In "I Just Wanna Testify" and "You Don't Miss Your Water" he comes to terms with the complex man who was his father. Short verses by Elvis Costello and William Bell introduce the reader to the major themes of this anthology. Information about the author and a section of excerpts from reviews in "Praise for the Poetry of Cornelius Eady" conclude the work.

36 Feelings, Tom, comp. and illus., *Soul Looks Back in Wonder*, ed. Maya Angelou, Dial Books, 1993 (hardcover), ISBN 0–8037–1001–1, unpaged, grades 7 and up.

Passionate and powerful artwork created in collage, stencil, spray-paint, and blueprint provides the foundation for this unique collection of poems. In his first full-color book, award-winning illustrator Tom Feelings has built on sketches he penned while on location in Ghana, Senegal, Guyana, and the United States. The artist then requested contributions from thirteen African American poets of renown, ranging from Langston Hughes, now deceased, to Darryl Holmes, the youngest contributor. The result is a stunning combination of text and illustration depicting a heritage rich in creativity. Most of the works are directed at the hope of the future—young adult readers. Walter Dean Myers likens the variance of the black experience to the ebb and flow of the Niger River in "History of My People." Haki R. Madhubuti issues challenges for change in "Destiny." Rashidah Ismaili expresses a deep love for the mother country in "Africa You Are Beautiful." A list of contributing authors opens the work. In an introductory essay, Feelings expresses his concern for contemporary youth and his desire that those of African descent know and cherish their heritage and value their creativity. Brief biographical sketches of the authors complete the anthology.

37 Fleming, Alice, comp., *Hosannah the Home Run! Poems about Sports*, Little Brown and Company, 1972 (hardcover), ISBN 0–316–28588–9, 68 pp., grades 6 and up.

If this small volume seems to speak to the twenty-first century adolescent in spite of its copyright date, it may be because the compiler credits her children with its inspiration. It may also be that subjects are so varied that there is something here for almost any sports enthusiast. In the thirty-four entries, individual and team activities from all seasons are included. Black and white photographs of athletes in action may date the work, but the verses are timeless. The twenty-nine contributors range from contemporary, such as William Carlos Williams, to the ancient Virgil and span the oceans. Robert Francis adds poetry to motion in "The Base Stealer." Humor from the sidelines prevails with "Dick

Szymanski" by Ogden Nash. Conrad Diekmann offers his own wry parody of Joyce Kilmer's classic verse in "Winter Trees." John Kieran celebrates the jolly danger of hockey in "There's This That I Like About Hockey, My Lad." Special features include a brief section entitled "Notes About the Poets" providing limited biographical information. An acknowledgments page precedes the text.

38 Fletcher, Ralph, *I Am Wings: Poems About Love*, photo. by Joe Baker, Bradbury Press, 1994 (hardcover), ISBN: 0–02–735395–8, 48 pp., grades 10 and up.

Few emotional experiences are as common to young adults as falling in and out of love. Like the two sides of an old-fashioned locket on a chain, this small treasure of a book opens to reveal both sides. Fletcher expresses all the delight, discovery, and adventure of finding love in his first chapter, aptly titled, "Falling In." Regret, recrimination, and lessons learned through loss make up chapter two, "Falling Out." Some of the verses represent responses from one section to the other as in "The Note" and "The Note Again," in which words wistfully spoken at one point turn and betray at another. In "Space" there is appreciation for a small imperfection that endears one to the other; however, in "Lies, Lies" something has broken in the relationship and the former beloved flaw becomes a missile to hurl at the hurt. The poems are not matched on a one-to-one ratio in the two sections, and some verses stand alone. All are masterfully written and nearly take away the breath of anyone who has ever been in love. These response poems are certain to draw passionate discussion and possibly unlock real creative writing among young adults.

Author Ralph Fletcher is also a consultant, working with teachers and students across the country to improve writing experiences in the classroom. He has written *Walking Trees* and *What a Writer Needs* to provide assistance for creative composition. Fletcher has also published two other volumes of poetry, *The Magic Nest* and *Water Planet*.

39 Fletcher, Ralph, *Ordinary Things: Poems from a Walk in Early Spring*, illus. by Walter Lyon Krudop, Atheneum Books for Young Readers, 1997 (hardcover), ISBN 0–689–81035–0, 48 pp., grades 6 and up.

Ralph Fletcher takes the reader with him on his daily walk along the road, through the woods, over the stream, and back. The observations he shares about the ordinary things of nature seen on the way lead the reader to more complex thoughts regarding his relationship to the world around. "Bird's Nests" recalls the wonder the author felt as a young boy when his grandmother threw his freshly cut hair on the ground so birds could weave it into their nest. "Stream" describes a place where tough decisions can be made. "Arrowhead" rouses dreams of those who peopled the land before. The thirty-three poems, artfully intermingled with the pencil sketches of Walter Krudop, are arranged one to a page. They are divided into three sections titled "Walking," "Into the Woods," and "Looping Back." The simple language makes the poems accessible, while the astute reflections encourage an awareness of the importance of everyday things we take for granted.

40   Fletcher, Ralph, *Relatively Speaking: Poems About Family*, illus. by Walter Lyon Krudop, Orchard Books, 1999 (hardcover), ISBN: 0–531–30141–9, 42 pp., grades 8 and up.

From the dedication to the final page, this volume is devoted to family—the good, the not-so-good, and the missing face. Readers begin their visit to the household with the youngest child, who serves as a guide throughout the book. Individual portraits painted in word pictures frame each family member as the reader is introduced to three generations, as well as girlfriends and cousins. Grandpa provides the climactic piece by posing questions regarding those ancestors who preceded even *him*. The young adult will be encouraged to reexamine family relationships, values, respect for the elderly, his own place in the whole concept of reunion, and the delight of extended family. Joy, grief, security, and a sense of identity are all concepts woven throughout this collection. For readers who are fortunate enough to have experienced family reunions, there will be a sense of nostalgia as they remember a time when they were younger, and the extended family may have framed their entire world. For the teen who has been mobile, disconnected by distance or parent's vocation, or is a member of a fractured family, there is a vicarious sense of what such times of coming together are all about.

Wide ranges of experiences are captured in verse. Foremost would be the everyday necessities, such as the common meals consumed around a kitchen table, as well as special events, including the stomach-stretching communal feasting that comprises family reunions. Doing chores and abiding by family rules and expectations are depicted as understood mores and are a part of what holds the family together. Another focus is the games—from the wild, exhilarating physical games like tag to the cross-generational sharing of a jigsaw puzzle—that has one piece missing, symbolizing a beloved cousin whose absence leaves the family mosaic incomplete. Finally, there are the more sensational events of death and a new birth—making the narrating youngest child no longer the holder of that distinction, but as one sage observer states, he has been "promoted." In a day when the family is struggling to find identity and purpose as a unit, Fletcher and Krudop have provided the missing piece for readers of all ages and of all families in this keepsake of a book. Making comparison to one's own parents and siblings and creative writing about family and social time with relatives will be natural outcomes of sharing these very personal verses.

41 Fletcher, Ralph, *Room Enough for Love: The Complete Poems of I Am Wings and Buried Alive*, Aladdin Paperbacks, n.d., (paperback) ISBN: 0–689–81976–5, 95 pp., grades 10 and up.

Subtitled "The Complete Poems from *I Am Wings* and *Buried Alive*," this pocket-sized volume represents both the joyous flight and the painful demise of young adult romance. Fletcher speaks so realistically of those breath-stopping heights and the unspeakable depths of first love and loss that the reader half expects him to step out from behind an adjacent locker door. His fresh and sensitive poems express the delight, agony, joy, and anger associated with finding or being found by the opposite sex during the precarious days when such relationships give definition to life.

The work is composed of two of Fletcher's previous books. His format is that of dialogue in which some poems respond to others; however, many stand alone. Titles are often proper names, and a story is told through the unspoken narrative from one poem to the next. An example is "Ted," a tough guy who can bench press more than he weighs. When an accident hospitalizes him, and he is ministered to by a petite candy striper, Ted's bravado takes flight, and he discovers that he is ready to commit his heart to her tiny hands. "Alexis" struggles with the chagrin and misery of her confusion over sexual orientation. "Dawne," who is pursued by a young man of a different race, has to watch a love note go up in smoke when her father discovers it. "Richard" leaves poignant memories when he moves away. "Brock" leaves behind a trail of unwanted pumpkins. The collection is completed by verses with provocative titles like "Suspicion," in which some strands of hair of a third party raise questions when found on a beach towel. "Not Fair" reveals the envy of the narrator, who has a crush on his little brother's baby-sitter. "It's Not About True Love" may help readers to see that shallow relationships are best ended.

This small collection would be useful in the classroom to introduce the power of a few words and the relevance of poetry to the life of many young readers. It would most certainly spark the creative urge to put on paper emotions that are throbbing around in the spirit. The only real disadvantage to using *Room Enough for Love* as a supplemental text is that volumes are certain to disappear.

42 Forrester, Victoria, *A Latch Against the Wind*, illus. by the author, Atheneum, 1985 (hardcover), ISBN 0–689–31091–9, unpaged, grades 6 and up.

Forrester's simple sketches are light and airy, a fitting accompaniment to her poems. Clear enough for sixth graders to understand, yet thoughtful enough for adults to ponder, these delicate verses are filled with delight in the joys of everyday life. Night and day are favorite themes in poems such as "At Hinge of Day" and "Sunset." Celebration of nature's seasons fills the lines of "Midsummer's Eve," and "I Hold October to My Eye." Above all, this poet extols the power of love in "So Penetrant a Light" and expresses awe at the gift of loving sacrifice in "Sometimes Our Feet Are Shepherd's Feet" and "Mending Stone." The beauty of expression draws the reader on from one poem to the next, demanding that each title receive its due.

43   Gaige, Amity, *We Are a Thunderstorm*, Landmark Editions, 1990 (hardcover), ISBN: 0–933849–27–3, 29 pp., grades 8 and up.

By the age of sixteen, Amity Gaige had already won numerous awards for her writing ability. Her talent spans the spectrum of literary genres. Prior to winning the 1989 National Written and Illustrated by . . . Awards Contest for *We Are a Thunderstorm*, Gaige had already published more than forty plays, essays, short stories, and poems. In this volume, the reader enjoys not only her writing talent but her perfectly matched photographs as well. Topics covered in this work represent a range of interests and emotions that should speak to any young person. Nature, family, beauty, cruelty, sadness, and joy framed in settings on land and sea await the reader. "Buttermints" expresses the simple ecstasy of being alive in autumn with a favorite candy to savor. "Trading" embraces the admiration/envy of two friends with culturally diverse hairstyles. "Encounter" evidences a brush with death in which both the teen and her father were survivors. "The Closet Monster" reflects on the agelessness of some fears. "The Writer" pays tribute to all those who try to capture life in words. Finally, the title poem recognizes individuals who band together to be heard and to achieve. Young adults will find themselves in these pages—in picture, in verse, or both. Gaige has created a timeless masterpiece, addressing ideas that touch all ages. Readers may even be inspired to create their own collection of Written and Illustrated by. . . .

44   Galloway, Owateka, *Revelations: The Power of Youth in Blue Jeans*, Coda Publications, 1999 (paperback), ISBN 0–910–39065–7, 96 pp., grades 10 and up.

If it seems that Galloway speaks authentically with the voice of youth, it is because she composed these verses while still a young adult. This volume of eighty-two poems is the first in the Blue Jeans series. From the denim-look of the cover to the back-pocket-sized paper-back, this small volume resonates with youthful attitudes. There are no chapter breaks, and verses have in common only the fact that each is a reflection of some aspect of life. "Laughter" ripples with joyous discoveries in the happiness of experiencing a good day. "Thank You to a Nastiness" pays powerful tribute to a relationship that is teaching life's hard lessons. "The Face" wrenches the heart with its intimate portrait of a homeless father. An index to first lines and a brief biographical annotation of the author complete the work.

45 Giovanni, Nikki, *Ego-Tripping and Other Poems for Young People*, illus. by George Ford, Lawrence Hill Books, 1993 (hardcover), ISBN 1–55652–189–X, 53 pp., grades 10 and up.

Nikki Giovanni's poems appear easy to read but unfold to many levels of meaning. They celebrate African American cultural and spiritual heritage, as in "For the Masai Warriors," while speaking directly to the harsh realities of life confronted by black youth expressed in "The Funeral of Martin Luther King, Jr." At the same time the poet addresses issues of interest to all young adults, such as loneliness in "Alone," dreams for the future in "Dreams," and the development of one's self-image in "Intellectualism." Divided into two sections, part one addresses political and social issues expressing unveiled anger at injustice and calling for political activism. Part two turns to subjects of a more personal nature. Language and subject matter make this book appropriate for older readers. Enhanced by the sepia-toned prints of George Ford, this edition adds ten titles to the original selection of twenty-two poems published under this same title. Virginia Hamilton strongly endorses the life and work of Giovanni in her supportive introduction. Those who enjoyed Giovanni's first edition may also wish to purchase this updated one. The table of contents provides the only access to the titles included.

46 Giovanni, Nikki, ed., *Shimmy Shimmy Shimmy Like My Sister Kate*, Henry Holt and Company, 1996 (hardcover), ISBN: 0–8050–3494–3, 186 pp., grades 9 and up.

Nikki Giovanni pays sparkling tribute to the Harlem Renaissance with her sensitive and insightful choice of writings by groundbreaking African American poets. In her comprehensive introduction, the author defines the time period, between 1917 and 1935, that provided rich and fertile soil for flowering of the arts in Harlem. Giovanni, highly respected in her own right, traces the trail of well-known pioneers in the arts and education. It is her goal in this slim volume to inspire others of her race to express themselves through the arts.

Beginning with the contributions of writers Paul Laurence Dunbar (1872–1906), W.E.B. DuBois (1868–1963), and others who predated the Harlem explosion, Giovanni moves through the verses of more than twenty black writers to the contemporary work of Ntozake Shange (1948–). Content covers topics as diverse as faith in "The Creation" by James Weldon Johnson, Melvin B. Tolson's finely tuned "Dark Symphony," and Countee Cullen's tribute to his African roots in "Heritage." Family relationships in the lovingly crafted "It is Deep" by Carolyn M. Rogers contrast with Ntozake Shange's searing depiction of sexual abuse in "It's Not So Good to Be Born a Girl/Sometimes." Both struggle and triumph are demonstrated in the variety of poems, and the entire range of emotions are given expression. Giovanni rounds out the collection with eight pages of informative biographical notes on each contributing poet including their life span, place of birth, and a listing of works. Additional information is provided in "Books for Further Reading," which chronicles anthologies and collections featuring more works of the contributing writers. This collection is unique in the variety of mood and content expressed by African American writers with similar experiences spanning nearly a century. It should provide encouragement for aspiring young writers to express themselves.

47 Giovanni, Nikki, *Those Who Ride the Night Winds*, William Morrow and Company, 1983 (hardcover), ISBN 0–688–01906–4, 62 pp., grades 10 and up.

Nikki Giovanni touches on a wide variety of subjects in these stream-of-consciousness selections. The famous names of Phillis Wheatly, Lorraine Hansberry, Robert F. Kennedy, and Martin Luther King, Jr., find places of honor here in verse. So do mothers, friends, and other loved ones. Two outstanding odes to love are found in "Reflections/On a Golden Anniversary" and "I Wrote a Good Omelet." In accessible yet thought-provoking lines, the author has poetically recorded her private observations of her personal life and of public happenings. The table of contents provides access to the poems, which vary in length from a few lines to three pages. The poet's preface, written in the same flowing style as the body of her work, addresses the place and the importance of poetry in culture.

48 Glaser, Isabel Joshlin, comp., *Dreams of Glory: Poems Starring Girls*, illus. by Pat Lowery Collins, Atheneum Books for Young Readers, 1995 (hardover), ISBN 0–689–31891–X, 47 pp., grades 6 and up.

Upbeat and encouraging, the thirty poems found in *Dreams of Glory* appeal to girls of many age levels. Divided into three sections titled "Sports," "Power," and "Dreams of Glory," verses such as "I Am Rose" and "Thumbprint," exude a confidence and positive assertion of identity. Expressions of determination, hope, and pride of accomplishment are found in titles like "74th Street" and "At the Pool." A desire to continue growing and improving finds voice in "The Finish Line." Many of the poets, such as Jean Little, Eve Merriam, Mel Glenn, and Cynthia Rylant, are familiar to poetry lovers and those knowledgeable about children's and young adult literature. The black and white portraits by Lowery Collins that introduce each section may appeal to the younger female more than to the young adult but the poems themselves display a broad enough range of depth and difficulty to satisfy the mature teen. A table of contents is the only listing of titles, but the brevity of the work makes other access unnecessary.

49 Glenn, Mel, *Back to Class*, photo. by Michael J. Bernstein, Clarion Books, 1988 (hardcover), ISBN 0–89919–656–X, 95 pp., grades 9 and up.

Glenn and Bernstein have collaborated to create a cast of believable teenage characters right out of the halls of Any High School, U.S.A. Bernstein's black and white photographs are, of course, of real students, but not with the same names as those immortalized by Glenn's poetry. Glenn states that it is his intention to create characters that seem so real that readers may look for them in the hall. In this collection there is more teacher influence than in *Class Dismissed* (1982). *Back to Class* provides a greater sense of the impact of those adults who meet young people in the classroom every day.

The collection of sixty-five free-verse pieces is not separated into chapters but rather by class periods and room numbers so that the reader gets a sense of the actual thoughts of students while occupying desks during a given class time. Interesting, also, are the varying feelings expressed by different students regarding the same assignment. When "Mr. Robert Winograd, English" (who has recently been told that he looks like an English teacher, and wonders just what that means) requires his students to write a composition about their future, students Luanne and Dennis respond from vastly different backgrounds. "Luanne Sheridan, Period 1" feels that before she can write about her future, she needs to fill in gaps about her past, like finding her biological mother. "Dennis Finch, Period 1" thinks he has very little control over his future, since his controlling father already has it mapped out for him. These are samples of the intriguing approach taken by Glenn as he creates his own small student body.

This creative approach to meeting teens where they live should open a myriad of doors to reader responses. The potential for original poetry based on selected classes, relationships with teachers, other classmates, and parents will be a natural outgrowth of this work. Even the use of Bernstein's photographs as springboards for other verses should start the creative juices flowing. This is one volume that will not gather dust on library shelves. An author's note opens the work, and brief biographical sketches conclude it.

50 Glenn, Mel, *Class Dismissed*, photo. by Michael J. Bernstein, Clarion Books, 1982 (hardcover), ISBN 0–89919–075–8, 96 pp., grades 10 and up.

Teenage angst changes little from one decade to the next. In this collection of verse, decorated with black and white photographs, Glenn and Bernstein record with authenticity those feelings that drive or inhibit young adults. Fictitious names serve as titles creating a feeling of intimacy with each character featured. "Marvin Pickett" extols the virtues of football. "Rhonda Winfrey" reveals the stomach-knotting stress that often plagues the overachiever. "Gail Larkin" reveals an unspoken dialogue that takes place with parents while very different desires are being expressed aloud. "Bernard Pearlman" injects some humorous thoughts from math class.

The table of contents reads like a class roster not yet alphabetized. There are no chapter breaks and only an occasional grouping of two or three entries connect with adjacent pieces. The seventy titles represent a balanced mix of ethnicity and gender. Although the collection may lack humor, it is, in general, representative of the emotional roller coaster ride that well represents young adult life.

51 Glenn, Mel, *Class Dismissed II: More High School Poems*, photo. by Michael J. Bernstein, Clarion, 1986 (hardcover), ISBN 0–89919–443–5, 96 pp., grades 10 and up.

Readers who have previously met Mel Glenn and Michael Bernstein's virtual yearbook of high school students in *Class Dismissed* and *Back to Class* will meet this third student body with great anticipation. Those who have not had the privilege of walking through fictitious halls with this team are in for an unforgettable experience. Glenn's free verse accompanied by Bernstein's photographs give such a realistic feel to these volumes that it is difficult to believe that the subjects don't attend the school just down the street. In this collection of seventy poems, most teen readers will find at least one verse that might spring right from the pages of their own lives. "Nolan Davis" struggles with identity issues as he first listens, then resists the voices of parents, teachers, and even friends. "Craig Blanchard" learns the real meaning of The Great Depression as he has a paper rejected because his teacher believes it is too good to be his. "Miguel De Vega" returns to school a year after graduation to show his principal what direction his life has taken. Insight pours out of these heartfelt lines that will enrich the understanding of parents and teachers. Teenagers, especially those who feel that no one understands their feelings, will find comfort in the fact that someone else has stood where they stand and survived. There are no chapter breaks. Created names serve as titles for each verse. Bernstein's black and white photographs, though made in the 1980s, are practically timeless.

52 Glenn, Mel, *Foreign Exchange: A Mystery in Poems*, Morrow Junior Books, 1999, ISBN: 0–688–16472–2 (hardcover), 157 pp., grades 10 and up.

In *Foreign Exchange* Mel Glenn has created a murder mystery, a who-done-it in verse, centered around the teens of rural Hudson Landing and urban Tower

High School. Inviting the city youth to visit their small town seems like a great idea to some members of the town council, while others fear they will bring crime, drugs, and all manner of evil. As teens from city and country are paired, the similarities of their problems and struggles become apparent. Both face the pressure of parental expectations, conflicting images of right and wrong, and the fears and jealousies of peer relationships. Unfolding the plot through free-verse reflections of a small town's adults and teens and their big-city visitors, Glenn reveals the desires, fears, angers, and prejudices that drive his characters. Ironically, while some feared the urban students would bring bad influences with them, the question arises, "Did the evil come from without or was the murderous intent already resident in the heart of one of Hudson Landing's own citizens?" The tone of this volume is dark. Though there are a few positive characters, it presents the negative side of most of the characters with little relief. While exposing the cultural and racial prejudices of his characters, Glenn nevertheless creates a tale full of stereotypes of his own. The verse is easy to read and touches on many issues with which teens may identify, such as relationships with parents and with the opposite sex, as well as their struggle to establish their own identity and their fears for the future. The desire to solve the mystery will keep them reading.

53 Glenn, Mel, *Jump Ball: A Basketball Season in Poems*, Lodestar Books, 1997 (hardcover), ISBN: 0–525–67–554–X, 160 pp., grades 8 and up.

Like an omniscient spectator, Mel Glenn both observes and reveals the spirits and souls of those most closely touched by a small-town basketball team. As the end of the season approaches and tensions mount, emotions prevail in the words of coach, teachers, parents, cheerleaders, spectators, bench-warmers, newscasters, and eventually, an undertaker. Like neighbors across a picket fence, readers find themselves eavesdropping on those to whom the game is more serious than life. Reaching out across the town, the sport draws in spectators who have little other excitement to brighten their lives and reluctantly includes teachers who think that the whole idea is a waste of time.

Like a coach in the huddle, Glenn selects his own plays in poetry. Taking rather a "zone" approach, he chooses rap, parody, and even concrete forms, most frequently following first person free verse for his narrative. Many of the characters speak more than once as the plot progresses, and by the end of the book, the reader feels as though he/she has watched the season from the sidelines. The smacking of the ball on the hardwood can be felt in the rhythm of these verses. Cheerleaders' chants punctuate each quarter and introduce the chapters.

Like the accomplished poet that he is, Mel Glenn speaks with the voice of contemporary young adults, sometimes using street language for power and effect. However, as he gives words to often unspoken feelings, he spans bridges that many adults are never able to cross. Readers may already know Glenn's work from his award-winning mystery in poems, *Who Killed Mr. Chippendale?* or his hostage drama in verse, *The Taking of Room 114*. As with his previous work, this is another book of poetry that readers will not want to put down. Foreshadowing lays the groundwork for an ending that will generate much discussion. For teachers who are looking for a collection of poetry that scores, *Jump Ball* is a slam-dunk.

54 Glenn, Mel, *My Friend's Got This Problem, Mr. Candler*, photo. by Michael J. Bernstein, Clarion Books, 1991 (hardcover), ISBN 0–89919–833–3, 103 pp., grades 10 and up.

Readers may feel that they are eavesdropping as they listen to hearts unburden in the office of Mr. Candler, the guidance counselor. Each verse has for its title the name of a student, parent, or grandparent who is demanding time, wisdom, or understanding from this school official. Chapters are designated by days of the week, and if entries are counted, it is not difficult to see that the counselor has a crowded schedule. Among those who cross Mr. Candler's threshold is a balance of gender and race. There are also telephone conversations from concerned adults who serve in the parental role. Although the characters are fictitious, problems represented are realistic and relevant. "Felicia Goodwin" wants advice on how to keep a love relationship without having sex. As "Wayne Buford" shares his lunch with Mr. Candler, he worries about how his family is going to survive since his dad lost his job. "Stephanie Royer" reveals the guilt she feels about being healthy while her little brother struggles with cancer. "Ramona Castillo" begins to talk about the haunting memories that left her an orphan. The connecting thread with each conference is that there is always a caring adult to listen. Michael Bernstein's black and white photographs add the finishing touch of reality to this provocative collection.

55 Glenn, Mel, *The Taking of Room 114: A Hostage Drama in Poems*, Lodestar Books, 1997 (hardcover), ISBN 0–525–67548–5, 182 pp., grades 10 and up.

As contemporary as tomorrow's headlines is this compelling story told in verse. The cast of characters includes students, faculty, parents, newscasters, and police. Although the setting is Tower High School, June 16th, some poems reflect thoughts of the students from their freshman through senior years. Rising action is based on the fact that Mr. Wiedermeyer's senior history class is being held hostage at gunpoint. Resolution comes as the police move in to disarm the obviously distraught teacher. Although few of these poems could be lifted out of context and appreciated individually, taken as a whole, there is a wealth of teaching ideas that spring from the entire body of work. Creative writing in poetry or prose is a possibility for the student with literary talents. Comparison of fact and fiction, analyzing perspective, and a study of news writing would meet the needs of the right-brained thinker.

There is some profanity and one voice reflects feelings of a homosexual male. However, taken as the suspense story it is, this book should reach even those students who have not previously demonstrated an interest in poetry. For those who already know its joys, this may become a favorite collection because it speaks with all voices—crossing age, gender, and ethnic lines. Special features include a class roster of students in Room 114 and a cast list of other characters.

56 Goldstein, Bobbye S., comp., *Inner Chimes: Poems on Poetry*, illus. by Jane Breskin Zalben, Boyds Mill Press, 1992 (hardcover), ISBN 1–56397–040–6, 24 pp., grades 6 and up.

For the teacher or parent who desires to transmit the magic of verse to students or to their own children, this small anthology is a treasure. Poetry is not defined here but rather is enjoyed in bits and pieces like the mosaics that reflect color in a kaleidoscope. Goldstein brings together the work of eighteen writers of renown, and Zalben's illustrations brighten each page. Mary O'Neill offers a veritable symphony of sounds with "Feelings About Words." Felice Holman bemoans the loss of the perfect verse with "The Poem That Got Away." Karle Wilson Baker expresses the illusive nature of the writing muse in "Days."

No chapter breaks are needed for this compact work. An acknowledgments page that lists sources may be used to locate other works by each of the contributors. A table of contents cataloging the twenty poems is the only other resource.

57 Gordon, Ruth, ed., *Peeling the Onion: An Anthology of Poems*, Harper Collins, 1993 (hardcover), ISBN 0–06–021727–8, 94 pp., grades 8 and up.

Comparing poetry to an onion, the editor points out several similarities between the two. As an onion can be peeled layer after layer, so can poetry be studied and enjoyed, revealing new discoveries at every level of meaning. Parts of an onion can be excerpted and replanted as can poetry, in order to glean new ideas. As with the pungent onion, cutting into a poem will often bring tears to the reader's eyes. Finally, just as the onion adds zest to food, so does poetry add zest to life, giving it a sharper, yet sweeter quality. The sixty-five titles chosen for this anthology show the excellent taste of the editor, including titles by Octavio Paz and Boris Pasternak. Writers such as Song Sun may be unfamiliar but nonetheless add quality to the whole. Nature is a recurrent theme as in "Watering the Garden" and "When I Heard the Learn'd Astronomer." Family relationships are explored as in "Braiding My Sister's Hair." Even humor is injected with "The Dirty-Billed Freeze Footy." Indexes of authors, titles, and first lines make the selections readily accessible.

58 Gordon, Ruth, comp., *Pierced by a Ray of Sun: Poems About the Times We Feel Alone*, Harper Collins Children's Books, 1995 (hardcover), ISBN 0–06–23614–0, 105 pp., grades 8 and up.

Since feelings of loneliness are universal, this collection will reach out like the ray in the title to all readers. Beginning with a succinct note to readers, Ruth Gordon draws in her audience from her opening sentences. What teenager has not experienced alienation from peers, parents, or even from themselves? Contributors come from all over the world. Yevgeny Yevtushenko, Gloria Fuertes, H. Leivick, and others have written in their native tongue but speak to the American readership through translators. A sampling of themes addressed are AIDS in "Elegy for John, My Student Dead of AIDS" (Robert Cording); having the courage to stand alone in "Fannie Lou Hamer"(Sam Cornish); teen pregnancy in "Pockets" (Katharyn Machan Aal); and special needs in "The One-Armed Boy" (Joseph Hutchinson). Many other topics are covered. Three indexes provide assistance in locating authors, titles, and first lines. There is a brief summary of the compiler's qualifications and accomplishments. Read straight through like a novel, this may be deemed a depressing collection. However, taken a few verses at a sitting, it meets a significant need of young adults in their times of feeling completely alone.

59 Gordon, Ruth, comp., *Time Is the Longest Distance*, Harper Collins, 1991, ISBN 0–06–022297–2, 74 pp., grades 9 and up.

Ruth Gordon has created a quality collection of poems centered on the passage of time. Many titles selected focus on time as it is measured off by the sunrise, the sunset, and the succession of seasons. Though a few are somber in tone, such as "Twilight," most are a celebration of nature and elicit an awareness of being a part of eternity. The cultural diversity of the sixty-one poems chosen make this a world anthology in a small volume. In addition to contributions by American and English authors, works have been translated from Chinese, French, Italian, Hebrew, Russian, Spanish, German, Japanese, and Yiddish. Although originating from many different countries, they are expressive of the yearnings, sadness, and joys common to all mankind and thus have universal appeal and encourage a sense of world community. All poems are one page or less in length and range in difficulty from simple to challenging. Helps to the reader include a short introduction and indexes to titles, authors, and the first lines of poems.

60   Hall, Donald, ed., *The Oxford Book of Children's Verse in America*, Oxford University Press, 1985 (hardcover), ISBN 0–19–503539–9, 319 pp., grades 5 and up.

Following in the tradition of Iona and Peter Opie's original *Oxford Book of Children's Verse*, Donald Hall has created an American version containing poems written for children and young adults, as well as those written for adults that children have adopted as their own. Selections were made from thousands of sources ranging from modern nonsense verse to Sunday School magazines of the past. The result is an eclectic anthology drawn from often-quoted authors and those virtually unknown to modern readers. From the wisdom of an astute squirrel in Emerson's "Fable," through the ethereal imagery of Carl Sandburg's "Fog," to the humorous wishes stated in Arthur Guiterman's "Ancient History," there lies a range of work that will allow teachers to incorporate poetry into any course in the curriculum. A time line of contributors would begin in the 1640s with *The Bay Psalm Book* and continue through Jack Prelutsky, who was born in 1940 and will most likely be publishing well into the twenty-first century. Selections are grouped by author and arranged by time periods from the 1600s to the present. Life-span dates are listed by the author's name in the table of contents.

In his expansive introduction, Hall defines the purpose and perimeters of an *Oxford Book of Children's Verse*. He states clearly that these do not necessarily represent his favorites, but rather those verses that represent the historical development of poetry for young people in America. Following the introduction and the body of the text, Hall has compiled ten pages of notes giving biographical summaries of the authors and informative annotations on other research sources used in the composition of the anthology. To complete the work there is an index of authors and an index of first lines and titles. For the teacher, librarian, parent, or any serious student of children's and young adult literature, this is an invaluable reference tool for classic American poetry. Its usefulness is not confined to the poetry, but for the supplemental material as well.

61   Harrison, David, *Wild Country: Outdoor Poems for Young People*, Wordsong/Boyds Mill Press, 1999 (hardcover), ISBN 1–56397–784–2, 48 pp., grades 6 and up.

Harrison's collection of forty-seven free verse nature poems is as refreshing as a walk in the woods. No illustrations clutter the pristine pages, and the reader's imagination is free to create its own scenes. The four chapters encompass different geographical regions and inspire both the academic and aesthetic audience. In the section entitled "Mountains" verses range in scope from the fragility of a fledgling in "Eaglet" to the power of weather in "Storm." In "Forest" the majesty of "Caribou" contrasts with the delicate splendor of "Butterflies." Chapters entitled "High Country" and "Sea" include hunters like "Mama Bear" and colorful clowns described in "Puffins." Beauty, joy, awe, and simplicity are all included in Harrison's tribute to the natural world. Adolescents from both rural and urban settings may take vicarious pleasure in these delightful visits to the outdoors. Each verse offers the reader its own special inspiration.

62 Harrison, Michael, and Christopher Stuart-Clark, comps., *The Oxford Treasury of Time Poems*, Oxford University Press, 1998 (hardcover), ISBN 0–19–276175–7, 155 pp., grades 7 and up.

To the adolescent, the most important time is the present. However, shaped by what has gone before and perhaps intrigued by visions of what is to come after, young adult readers will find this collection one to ponder and return to again and again. Selections include more than one hundred works from classic writers of verses for children and adults from both sides of the Atlantic. Of the seventy-six contributors, many are from the British Isles including Shakespeare, Dylan Thomas, and Seamus Heaney. Poems are grouped into eleven chapters, each bearing a title focusing on some aspect of time. Christina Rossetti introduces the work with "How Many?" reminding readers of the limitless nature of time. Emily Dickinson writes wonderingly, "Will There Really Be a Morning?" James Weldon Johnson offers his vision of "The Creation." Jenny Joseph adds a smile to thoughts of aging with "Warning." Concluding visions include those by Robert Frost in "Fire and Ice" and the biblical prophet, Micah, in "The Last Days."

A variety of artistic expression, ranging from delicate black and white illustrations to colorful collages, adorns each page and showcases the talents of ten different artists. Special features include an index of titles and first lines combined, an index of authors, an index of artists, and an acknowledgments page. This is a versatile collection because of the variety of topics and will quickly become a favorite with teachers and students alike.

63 Harrison, Michael, and Christopher Stuart-Clark, eds., *A Year Full of Poems*, Oxford University Press, 1991 (hardcover), ISBN 0–19–276097–1, 141 pp., grades 7 and up.

Just as the impact of seasons, months, holidays, and weather can be shared across age, culture, and gender barriers, so can this anthology be shared. Grouped in twelve chapters corresponding to the calendar, this collection provides a poem for almost every occasion. More than eighty-five authors with styles as varied as that of Elizabeth Coatsworth and James Berry are represented. Each page spread is decorated by a black and white or full color illustration representing a range of styles from thirteen artists, with Valerie McBride showcased on the jacket and thirteen other pages. Although this collection would not be classified as adolescent literature, most pieces will connect with that audience. Middle schoolers will find themselves in the center of the action in "He Who Owns the Whistle Rules the World" by Roger McGough. For the teen who has summer to spend in the country, "Timeless" by Judith Nicholls will hold nostalgic charm. Wes Magee creates a shaky shape poem expressing the angst of teen scholars approaching the first day of school in "Are You Ready?" Irene Thompson focuses on the dark beauty of the city in "Rainy Nights." Charlotte Zolotov's closing poem "Change" identifies exactly who it is that is in transition. This versatile collection, with its stress on the rhythm of life, has the potential to become a favorite of the young adult audience. Indexes to authors, artists, titles, and first lines assist readers in finding specific information. An acknowledgments page lists resources for each entry.

64 Harvey, Anne, comp., *Shades of Green*, illus. by John Lawrence, Greenwillow Books, 1991 (hardcover), ISBN 0–688–10890–3, 192 pp., grades 9 and up.

Those searching for literature to complement a study of the environment may find *Shades of Green* to be a helpful additional resource. Divided into ten sections, the collection of around two hundred nature poems celebrates all things green, from grass to flowers, to trees, to insects and even frogs. Crying out against the encroachment of concrete and asphalt on field and forest, titles in the chapter "Goodbye to Hedges" voice a strong concern for our environment. "Rings of Grain," "He Praises the Trees," and "So They Are Felled" are chapters that focus on the beauty and importance of trees to our well-being. Humble grass and weeds are given their due in selections from "The Grass Is Green," and "Flower-Lovers and Weed-Lovers."

The illustrations, though lovely, give the collection the appearance of a book for younger children. Conversely, some of the poems are more flowery and more difficult than many teens will appreciate. The British setting of a large number of selections will be unfamiliar to American teens. In spite of these factors, the collection as a whole encourages young people to observe the world around them more closely and with greater respect and appreciation. An introduction by the authors sets the tone of the book. Indexes are provided for first lines of poems, titles, and authors.

65 Hearne, Betsy, *Polaroid and Other Poems of View*, photo. by Peter Kiar, Collier Macmillan, 1991 (hardcover), ISBN 0–689–50530–2, 68 pp., grades 9 and up.

Stating in her foreword that, "poetry is a way of seeing," Hearne focuses on viewing familiar scenes of life from new perspectives. Observing the arrival of dusk, a spring rain, or a city street become more intense experiences for readers as the poet exposes them to her insight. Young people who have lived through their parents' divorce might identify with the feelings expressed in "Geology." Relationships take center stage in "Sisters" and "Learning Loving." Resisting the efforts of society to squeeze everyone into expected roles is the theme of "For Whom the Glass Slipper Did Not Fit." Titles are divided into seven sections: "Outside," "City Sights," "Close-ups," "Insights," "Second Sight," "Dark and Light," and "Long View." Access to the forty-seven poem titles is through the table of contents. Photographs that introduce each section reflect the tone of the poems to come.

66 Herrick, Steven, *Love Ghosts and Nose Hair: A Verse Novel for Young Adults*, University of Queensland Press, 1996 (paperback), ISBN: 0–7022–2878–8, 115 pp., grades 7 and up.

Love Ghosts and Nose Hair, a story in verse, is about real love, the ghost of a wife and mother, and nose hair—both real and metaphorical. As the story unfolds, sixteen-year-old Jack, his worldly wise older sister, Desiree, and their widowed father take on vivid personalities. Each has a distinct voice as they speak of the loss of their mom or wife, sex, and most importantly, relationships. Each family member struggles with grief independently, not wanting to hurt the others. As life moves on there are other concerns as well. Initially, Jack has many questions—mostly about sex and how he might go about experiencing it. Desiree shares sisterly knowledge and advice but informs him that to discover all he wants to know he must have a partner. Dad is dangerously close to alienating his children as he turns more often to alcohol to fill the void created when his beloved wife died of cancer. Readers can gauge the affection in this family though the verse, "The Cubby House." The little playhouse really should be torn down but when Jack and his dad go to demolish it, they decide instead to go to town and buy paint.

The plot emerges as pages turn and intimacy is established with each of the trio. Dad writes of his now dead dreams in "The Family Team." Desiree writes in "Desiree" of nightly examining her breasts in search of a lump like the one that sounded the death knell for her mother. By the final verses, Jack has found his own answers to his earlier questions about sex as he expresses in "The Right Reasons." Though Steven Herrick writes with Australian vocabulary, his themes are universal—love, coming of age, family, grief, loss, and making choices. Since Jack is dealing with awakening sexuality, some poems are rather frank in their treatment of the topic. Therefore, the adult who plans to share this book with teens will want to plan ahead for the wisest use of the contents. Herrick successfully brings the reader to the ghost level as he issues an invitation to move through the household, allowing intimate access to each member—even "Mum."

67 Hill, Helen, Agnes Perkins, and Alethea Helbig, comps., *Straight on Till Morning: Poems of the Imaginary World*, illus. by Ted Lewin, Thomas Y. Crowell, 1977 (hardcover), ISBN O–690–01303–5, 150 pp., grades 8 and up.

Although this collection is classified as one for children, there are a number of verses that the young adult reader will enjoy as well. The compilers have chosen works based on their significant number of years in the classroom. These pieces are designed to spark creative thoughts among readers, whatever the age, through poems of mystery, legend, humor, and above all imagination. The nearly one hundred poems are divided into eight chapters with groupings based on themes. The list of forty-nine contributors reads almost like a hall of fame for writers of literature for children and young adults. May Swenson suggests a philosophical look at the sky as a metaphor for life in "The Cloud-Mobile." J.R.R. Tolkien stimulates thoughts of the mystical world with "Shadow-Bride." Emily Dickinson asks the question that is a constant with teens, "I'm Nobody, Who Are You?" Theodore Roethke sends chills up the spine with his eerie approach to "The Small." Fourteen pages of annotations supply biographical information of the contributors. Indexes of poets, titles, and first lines and an acknowledgments page complete the volume. Pen and ink sketches by Ted Lewin add fragile beauty throughout the work.

68 Hirschfelder, Arlene B., and Beverly R. Singer, eds. *Rising Voices: Writings of Young Native Americans*, Macmillan Publishing Company, 1992 (hardcover), ISBN 0–684–19207–1, 115 pp., grades 8 and up.

Beverly Singer, who learned to write in a Bureau of Indian Affairs day school, joins Arlene Hirschfelder in compiling poetry and essays by young Native Americans. The goal of this collection was to let the youth of this particular group speak about themselves, their families, and their futures. Careful selection was made from numerous works. Both artistry and accuracy were criteria. The finished product showcases writers ranging in age from eleven to nineteen across nearly a century. Fourteen states from Alaska to Arizona and from Maine to Mississippi are represented. Voices of more than thirty tribes speak out, from Aleuts to Zunis. The anthology is composed of six divisions in both poetry and prose. Chapter titles include "Identity," "Family," "Homelands," "Ritual and Ceremony," "Education," and "Harsh Realities." Following each piece is a brief biographical note providing name, tribe, location of the writer, and previous publication information. An acknowledgments page lists alphabetically the title and author of each entry. An author/title index completes the work.

69 Holbrook, Sara, *The Dog Ate My Homework*, Boyds Mill Press, 1996 (paperback), ISBN 1–56397–638–2, 47 pp., grades 6–8.

Holbrook creates a collection of verse that speaks with that in-between voice of the middle schooler. The cover, featuring the destructive canine of the title, appeals to teacher and student alike. Most of the thirty-five free verse pieces mirror some aspect of school and will fit nicely into that crucial space of time just after the bell rings and before focus shifts to the subjects of the day. Topics chosen by the author indicate her knowledge of adolescent life and times. The relative unimportance of being tardy when weighed against arrival *at all* is stated in "Swimming Upstream." Feelings of betrayal at having secrets exposed are expressed in "You Promised." Discovery of what separates those who succeed from those who fail is revealed in "Winners." Each of the brief poems addresses some aspect of being at an age when parents and teachers often expect maturity but give responses more appropriate to a child. Perhaps it is in these years that poetry may be the most effective tool of communication.

70 Holbrook, Sara, *Feelings Make Me Real*, Kid Poems, 1990 (paperback), ISBN 0–999–00777–7, 46 pp., grades 6–10.

Sara Holbrook's poems seem to be able to capture the feelings behind life's triumphs and disappointments, its joys and its fears. The poems are written specifically for young people and resonate with truth for anyone who has survived the pangs of growing up. What person has not experienced the despair expressed in "I Hate My Body"? After a disagreement over how to do something, who has not wanted to say "My Way is Better"? Who has not wallowed, if even for a moment, in the self-pity expressed in "The Loneliest," or "Misery"? With deftness of touch, Holbrook uses humor to lighten the impact while touching on areas of real pain. These thirty-seven concise bits of wisdom—tempered by wit—are presented without illustration. Access to the titles is provided by the table of contents.

71 Holbrook, Sara, *I Never Said I Wasn't Difficult*, Boyds Mill Press, 1996 (paperback), ISBN 1–56397–639–0, 48 pp., grades 8 and up.

From the title that may elicit both smiles and tears from parents and teachers on through the final poem, Sara Holbrook chronicles the roller coaster ride that depicts young adulthood. Focusing on topics that run the gamut from pain and depression to love and acceptance, these thirty-seven small verses touch all emotions. "The Storm That Was" will seem very familiar to parents who have listened while their children explode through a crisis. "A Step" describes that defining moment in a date—returning to the front door. "Hammock Talk" reminds readers that it is permissible, even desirable, to spend *some* time alone and relaxed. "Attention Seeking" voices the fear of all who feel rejection. The verses in this thin volume allow young adults to discover that they are not alone in the alienation they often experience during the nebulous teen years. This little masterpiece is one that students will want to return to again and again. They may even *choose* to memorize and quote their favorites.

72 Holbrook, Sara, *Nothing's the End of the World*, illus. by J.J. Smith-Moore, Wordsong/Boyds Mills Press, 1995 (hardcover), ISBN 1–56397–249–2, 48 pp., grades 5 and up.

No matter what the age of the reader, everyone will identify with at least one situation presented so humorously in Holbrook's *Nothing's the End of the World*. Life's little embarrassments and annoying difficulties become times to laugh about in poems like "Bad Joke" and "This Can't Be." The puzzlements of amorous endeavors are made amusing in "Why Do They Call That Love?" With so many serious issues at stake during adolescent years, Holbrook brings welcome comic relief and reminds readers that in spite of the fact that they may have received the worst haircut in the world, or have been told they have to wear braces, life does go on. J.J. Smith's comic-strip-style illustrations emphasize the humor of the verse.

73 Holbrook, Sara, *Walking on the Boundaries of Change*, Boyds Mill Press, 1998 (paperback), ISBN 1–56397–737–0, 64 pp., grades 8 and up.

In this flawless little book subtitled "Poems of Transition," Sara Holbrook explores some of the most significant issues faced by young adults. She addresses new experiences, difficult choices, and a search for truth with the wisdom of a mother and teacher while keeping intact the teen perspective. The title piece defines friendship. "A Choice" provides a manifesto for parent/child communication. "Homecoming" humorously reveals the disparity in gender values for that great social event. "Blown Away" vividly depicts the downward spiral of a would-be leader who has become a carbon copy follower. Holbrook pours much insight into these fifty-three brief verses. The profound simplicity of each poem begs for discussion, collection, written response, and even memorization. For any middle or high school teacher who desires a collection that speaks to the feelings of every student, this is a "must have."

74 Hopkins, Lee Bennett, *Been to Yesterdays: Poems of a Life*, illus. by Charlene Rendeiro, Wordsong/Boyds Mills Press, 1995 (hardcover), ISBN 1–56397–467–3, 64 pp., grades 6–10.

Useful in the study of autobiography and poetry, this volume begins with an image of "a picture-perfect family." From that starting point, Hopkins takes the reader through a year full of turmoil and loss. He gives expression to the feelings of a young person whose seemingly secure and loving family is torn apart by "bitter, brutal words" that become that "dreaded word—divorce." He chronicles the struggle of a single parent trying to raise children alone and exposes the fear caused in the child by the specter of alcoholism. Adding to this already substantial volume of difficulty is the death of a grandmother and the loss of her sustaining love. The last pages of Bennett's saga do not end in despair, however, but in a prayer for strength and with a decision to become a writer. Except for one quoted nursery rhyme, the author manages to condense this tumultuous year into twenty-eight short poems. No line of these verses contains more than five words. Most have only one or two. This simple style should encourage young people to believe that they too can effectively express their experiences on paper.

75 Hopkins, Lee Bennett, comp., *Hand in Hand: An American History through Poetry*, illus. by Peter M. Fiore, Simon and Schuster, 1994 (hardcover), ISBN 0–671–73315–X, 144 pp., grades 6 and up.

Lee Bennett Hopkins has chosen more than seventy-five poems to tell the story of America. Beginning with the arrival of the *Mayflower* in 1620 and culminating with space flight in the twentieth century and predictions for the years beyond, selections unfold the adventure of discovery, settling, and venturing further. Chapter titles depict the themes and eras covered in their pages. In "Ring! Oh, Ring for Liberty," writers such as Henry Wadsworth Longfellow with his, "Paul Revere's Ride" and Laura E. Richards with "Molly Pitcher" celebrate the brave deeds of our founding fathers and mothers. In "Riding To and From," Carl Sandburg pays tribute to rural life in "Illinois Farmer," while E.B. White muses on the life of a suburban dweller in "Commuter." Isabel Joshlin Glaser gives food for thought on cross-cultural relations in "The Last Good War—and Afterward." Forty-five writers from traditional through contemporary and on to those who are publishing for the first time contribute to this collection. Peter M. Fiore's soft illustrations blend perfectly with the text. A table of contents; introduction; acknowledgments page; and indexes of titles, first lines, and authors complete the text.

76 Hopkins, Lee Bennett, comp., *Love and Kisses*, illus. by Kris Boyd, Houghton Mifflin Company, 1984 (paperback), ISBN 0–395–34554–5, 48 pp., grades 10 and up.

The title sums up the contents of this single subject anthology. Thoughts of love—new, old, lost, and found—are shared by more than twenty contemporary writers. Length of the twenty-five entries ranges from the twenty-one line narrative creation from "Hooking Up" by Richard Thomas to the brief but beautiful "You" penned by Prince Redcloud. Viewpoints vary from Maya Angelou's lonely musings in "Greyday" to Nikki Giovanni's celebration of a day apart in "A Certain Peace." Love at any stage is given voice in this anthology. There are no chapter breaks. The only special feature is an acknowledgments page that serves to conclude the volume.

77 Hopkins, Lee Bennett, comp., *My America: A Poetry Atlas of the United States*, illus. by Stephen Alcorn, Simon and Schuster Books for Young Readers, 2000 (hardcover), ISBN 0–689–81247–7, 83 pp., grades 6–10.

America of the past and the present blend together in this collection of fifty poems arranged by geographic region. From the buoy bells of Bar Harbor, Maine, to the fire-breathing mountain of Mauna Loa, Hawaii, the diversity of these United States is portrayed with understanding and appreciation. The pulsating life of "Tonight in Chicago" is loved as much as the "Front Porch" of the small town Midwest. Verse extolling our natural landmarks, such as "For Purple Mountains' Majesty," stand alongside those exploring the routines of daily life, as in "Seattle Morning." More than providing a geography lesson, poets have captured in word the hopes and dreams of the American people. Stephen Alcorn's bright, textured works, interpreting and enlarging the messages of the poets, adorn every page. Sectional maps and factual highlights of each state make this volume a useful support for history lessons. Most of the names, such as Langston Hughes, X.J. Kennedy, and Carl Sandburg, will be familiar to readers. Twenty of the works were commissioned specifically for this collection. Indexes to authors, titles, and first lines make the poems easily accessible.

78 Hopkins, Lee Bennett, ed., *My Mane Catches the Wind*, illus. by Sam Savitt, Harcourt Brace Jovanovich, 1979 (hardcover), ISBN 0–15–256343–1, 42 pp., grades 6 and up.

Students who are horse lovers will surely find something to please in this tribute to horses of all kinds. Beginning with "The Birth of a Foal," entries move through the strong days of maturity to end with "The Prayer of the Old Horse." The sketches of Sam Savitt bring life to verses by authors from Europe,

Asia and, the United States. An index of authors, titles, and first lines is provided along with a profile of the editor and the illustrator.

79 Hopkins, Lee Bennett, comp., *Opening Days*, illus. by Scott Medlock, Harcourt, Brace and Company, 1996 (hardcover), ISBN 0–15–200270–7, 35 pp., grades 4 and up.

The poems of *Opening Days* are short, straightforward celebrations of physical activity. Well-known names of adolescent literature such as Lillian Morrison, Gary Soto, and Arnold Adoff appear along with less familiar poets. Hopkins himself contributes two selections. The oil on paper paintings of Scott Medlock add color and beauty to the picture-book layout. These illustrations encompass all ages from the sandlot baseball player to the professional athlete. Sports include the team activities of basketball, soccer, and football as well as the individual pursuit of activities like bicycling, tennis, and skiing. Eighteen poems express the joy and sometimes agony of twelve sports. No index is needed.

80 Hughes, Judith E., *Betty and Rita Go to Paris*, photo. by Michael Malyszko, Chronicle Books, 1999 (hardcover), ISBN 0–8118–2370–9, 83 pp., grades 6 and up.

French teachers take note. Two irresistible traveling Labradors are available to guide your students on a whimsical tour of the City of Lights. Their visits to the famous sites of la fontaine Stravinski, Notre-Dame, and la place St. Michel are chronicled by Judith Hughes in canto-centric verse and photographed by Michael Malyszko. Besides the tourist destinations, the lovable pooches find time to visit *un café, un bistro* and *un boucher*. Vocabulary and culture both are introduced with a light touch.

81 Hughes, Langston, *The Block*, illus. by Romare Bearden, selected by Lowery S. Sims and Daisy Murray Voigt, intro. by Bill Cosby, Metropolitan Museum of Art, Viking, 1995 (hardcover), ISBN 0–670–86501–X, 32 pp., grades 6 and up.

Blending the word mastery of Langston Hughes and the skill of Romare Bearden with paper and paint, *The Block* creates a tribute to the neighborhood that nurtured these two great artists of American culture. In matching sections of Bearden's six-panel collage, with verse by Hughes, the sights and sounds of Harlem are brought vividly to life, almost like scenes in a movie. The bold colors and arresting designs used on the pages match the vibrancy of the original work, which is presented in a double-page spread on the title pages. The picture-book size and format of this volume is deceiving, for the text is definitely attuned to older readers. For those who have lived in similar settings, this volume will stir feelings of recognition. For those who have not, it can provide an exposure to the realities of urban life. An introduction written by Bill Cosby prefaces the book, and full-page biographies of author and artist bring it to a close.

82   Hughes, Langston, *The Dream Keeper and Other Poems*, illus. by Brian Pinkney, Scholastic Inc., 1994 (paperback), ISBN 0–590–62396–6, 83 pp., grades 6 and up.

First published in 1932, this collection was chosen by Hughes himself to be published in a volume specifically for young people. His only collection designated as such, the poems nonetheless portray themes that are universal to all ages and times. "Poem" touches on the sadness of losing a friend. "April Rain Song" describes the joy of a soft spring rain. Many of Hughes' poems came out of his blackness and, like "The Negro" and "I, Too," echo the pride he had in his race. Others, like "Merry-Go-Round," express the struggle and frustration of striving for equality. The thrust of this collection, summarized in "Dream," is the important relationship between holding on to dreams and the quality of life. *The Dream Keeper* is introduced by well-known anthologist Lee Bennett Hopkins and ends with a personal note by Augusta Baker, a close friend who was storyteller-in-residence at the University of South Carolina. Woodcut illustrations are provided by award-winning artist Brian Pinkney. Its short poems are a powerful commentary on life in America and would be useful in any classroom.

83   Hull, Robert, comp., *Breaking Free: An Anthology of Human Rights Poetry*, Thompson Learning, 1995 (hardcover), ISBN 1–56847–196–3, 64 pp., grades 10 and up.

Freedom wears as many faces as there are countries to celebrate it. To the young adult, freedom may simply mean having his driver's license. This collection will serve to enlarge his vision. Robert Hull has selected verses that explore both freedom-to and freedom-from. These concepts are clearly explained in his introduction. The forty-six poems included in the anthology represent freedom lost or found in countries around the world. Many pieces are translations from oppressed people whose spirits refuse to die. Virginia Driving Hawk Sneve revels in the joy of natural freedom in "I Watched an Eagle Soar." W.H. Auden speaks of the pain of loss in "Refugee Blues." Bruce Dawe, in "Description of an Idea," and Bertolt Brecht, in "The Democratic Judge," shine lights of inspiration and hope as they celebrate the flame of undying hope residing in the human spirit. No chapter breaks confine the poems. Some verses are translated out of their original languages of Greek, Spanish, Chinese, German, or more than ten others. Contributors range from well-known writers Pablo Neruda and Langston Hughes to an eight-year-old child. Special features include an introduction to open the work and explanatory notes at the conclusion. An index of first lines and page numbers make each work more easily accessible.

84 Janeczko, Paul B., *Brickyard Summer*, illus. by Ken Rush, Orchard Books, 1989 (hardcover), ISBN 0–531–05846–8, 53 pp., grades 8 and up.

These poems open a window on summer in a small New England town as seen through the eyes of a young adolescent male. Besides baseball and time spent with a best friend, this season brings a dawning awareness of some of life's more difficult issues such as aging, in "Reverend Mona," death in "Brothers," and homelessness in "Walker." There is also an awakening to the future promise of a different kind of relationship with girls in "The Kiss." Anyone who has grown up in a small town may recognize the personalities and the experiences of this way of life. The rather crude black and white paintings of Ken Rush provide a strong accent to these irreverent, yet winsome poems.

85 Janeczko, Paul B., ed., *The Crystal Image: A Poetry Anthology*, Dell Publishing, 1992 (paperback), ISBN 0–440–91553–8, 159 pp., grades 9 and up.

Paul Janeczko's ability to find poems with a satisfying depth of imagery that remain clear and precise shines in this collection of titles appropriate for young adults. Widely diverse styles are found in poems that depict the powerful forces that shape our lives. Theodore Roethke's "The Big Wind" showcases nature's potentially destructive force. "Love Come Quietly" by Robert Creeley attests to the strength of the soft, but equally intense powers of love. Memories of everyday events of the past wield a strong influence on present-day life in D.H. Lawrence's "Piano." Grouped into nine chapters, themes include "The World Around Us," "Sports," "Places/Things," "Glad Love," "Sad Love," "Aloneness," "Young People," "Past Youth," and "Death." Lee Bennett Hopkins' introduction serves to open the reader's mind to the place and purpose of poetry in his or her own life as well as to provide an entrance to the more than one hundred titles to come. Thirteen pages of acknowledgments and three pages of table of contents precede the collection itself. An index of authors is given at the back.

86 Janeczko, Paul B., ed. *Don't Forget to Fly*, Bradbury Press, 1981 (hardcover), ISBN 0–87888–187–5, 144 pp., grades 9 and up.

This collection, an early work for Paul Janeczko, groups together poems by topics from sunrise to suicide. More than fifty contemporary writers have contributed to this work, with an introductory piece by Walt Whitman. Most are in free verse form. A sampling of titles and their creators provides an overview of the breadth of the anthology. Langston Hughes contributes an intimate view of one's final thoughts in "Suicide's Note." Eve Merriam touches all the senses in "Love Letters, Unmailed." Robert Hayden in "Those Winter Sundays" and Richard Shelton in "Letter to a Dead Father" portray opposing views of parental experiences. Karl Shapiro shares a rousing tribute to his car in "Buick." Special features include an acknowledgments page, giving the source for each entry, and an index of poets. This collection will be especially useful in demonstrating to students that perspective affects creative expression, and that in life there is always more than one way to view an object, a person, or a relationship.

87 Janeczko, Paul B., ed., *Going Over to Your Place*, Bradbury Press, 1987 (hardcover), ISBN 0–02–747670–7, 159 pp., grades 10 and up.

The tone of the collection gathered by Janeczko in *Going Over to Your Place* is melancholy and thoughtful. They are strong poems that mourn lost love and focus on alienation between parents and children. The emotional adjustments of moving to a new place and the accompanying sense of loss are expressed in "Note to the Previous Tenants." Death reigns in "For a friend," and "The One to Grieve." Broken hearts take center stage in "The Departure," and "This Love." One noted digression from solemnity to humor is Jenny Joseph's "Warning" about her bold approach to aging. A number of these poems are adult in focus but there are sufficient titles of universal appeal that make this anthology useful in the classroom. Particularly thought-provoking for group discussion are "The Amputee Soldier," and "He Sits Down on the Floor of a School for the Retarded." Although he has not labeled the titles by topic, Janeczko nevertheless has clustered his choices by general subject areas and divided them into four parts. The only other guide to the collection is an index to poets.

88 Janeczko, Paul B., ed., *Home on the Range: Cowboy Poetry*, illus. by Bernie Fuchs, Dial Books, 1997 (hardcover), ISBN 0–8037–1911–6, 38 pp., grades 8 and up.

This unique anthology recognizes a profession that is almost as old as the nation itself. Compiled by award-winning poet, writer, editor, and teacher Paul Janeczko, these nineteen poems capture the freedom of the cowboy spirit. In support, Bernie Fuchs reflects the mood of each verse with majestic illustrations. Readers who long for the freedom of the open plains or those who are fascinated by the dangers of the lonely trail will take vicarious pleasure in these poems. Content varies from lonely ballads to humorous verses. Many contemporary cowboy poets are represented. Red Stegall expresses the dependability of the range rider in "Hats Off to the Cowboy." Virginia Bennett explains the motivation for hard work in "You Probably Know This Guy." Vess Quinlan compares the corporate ladder to the chores of a country boy in "The Barn Cats." Finally, Robert Fletcher bids farewell to days long gone in "The Trail of an Old Timer's Memory." This collection is especially significant because of the contribution made to the country by the independence, diligence, and perseverance of the men and women here honored in illustration and rhyme. Most young adult readers may have very little knowledge of the actual day-to-day demands met by these stalwarts, but their example is well worth emulation.

89   Janeczko, Paul B., ed., *Looking for Your Name: A Collection of Contemporary Poems*, Orchard Books, 1993 (hardcover), ISBN 0–531–086259, 143 pp., grades 9 and up.

Janezcko has gathered together one hundred twelve poems by eighty-six different poets whose subjects are as varied as life itself. The volume is divided into two sections with the first one touching on "public" experiences that effect society as a whole. George Ella Lyons comments on ecology in "Stripped," as does Leo Dangel's "Restoring the Ecology." James Nolan makes observations about technology in "Modern Times," a theme that Alice Fulton echoes in "When Bosses Sank Steel Islands." Seven poems explore the effects of war, including Robert Morgan's "Vietnam War Memorial" and Liz Rosenberg's "What Holds Us Back." The second section deals with "private" issues, concentrating on the inner conflicts of mind and heart. Christine Hemp and Robert Louthan examine the struggles of dealing with another person's death in "Even When," and "The Most Haunted," respectively. Parent and child relationships are the issues in "Winter Stars" by Larry Lewis, and touching on a theme relevant to the lives of many contemporary adolescents is Lee Sharkey's "The Absent Father." For young adults struggling to know themselves, Mark Vinz has penned "Eye of the Beholder." In *Looking for Your Name*, Janeczko has created a small, fully indexed anthology dealing with universal issues that trouble not only teens but people of all ages.

90   Janeczko, Paul B., ed., *The Music of What Happens: Poems That Tell Stories*, Orchard Books, 1988 (hardcover), ISBN 0–531–05757–7, 188 pp., grades 10 and up.

"What happens" in this anthology is life—fresh, uncluttered, sometimes raw, Life. These seventy-five story poems unleash plot, characterization, theme, rising action, and resolution as surely as a comparable collection of short stories. There are no chapter breaks to separate the flow of thought, yet each poem stands alone. Well known for his numerous contributions to young adult literature,

Janeczko does not disappoint readers in this volume. He has chosen eclectic contributions from Hawaii (Garrett Hongo) to Appalachia (Jim Wayne Miller and George Ella Lyon). The humor of Leo Dangel's "Gathering Strength" and "The New Lady at Ralph's Barber Shop" and the pathos of Stephen Dunn's "The Sacred" strike emotional notes. There are themes rising from the rural heartland as in "Close to Home" by Frank Steele and those reflecting feelings of city-dwelling, first-generation immigrants in Gregory Djanikian's "How I Learned English." For the student who finds reading or writing poetry disconnected from his or her life experiences, this volume brings connection. For mature readers, who find freedom of expression in reading and composing verse, this collection provides fresh viewpoints and may inspire potential poets to compose their own "music."

91 Janeczko, Paul B., ed., *The Place My Words Are Looking For*, Bradbury Press, 1990 (hardcover), ISBN 0–02–747671–5, 150 pp., grades 6 and up.

For those who have found writing poetry to be a passionate puzzle, this anthology will be a refreshing delight. Thirty-nine of the finest contemporary writers for adults, young adults, and children share their thoughts on the process of composing their work along with sample pieces. They also graciously give glimpses into their personal lives. Readers discover how childhood and adolescent adventures, aspirations, dreams, and heartaches of these authors have been translated into verses that connect with their vast audience. Here is a small sampling of the contents. Naomi Shihab Nye believes that one value of poetry lies in the fact that it causes the reader to take life slowly and listen to its rhythms. In her offering, "The Rider," Nye addresses the issue of loneliness. Lillian Morrison sees the essential ingredient of poetry to be that of capturing a special moment, or memory, whether it is real or imagined. Her vehicle for demonstrating this idea is "The Sidewalk Racer" and "On the Skateboard."

J. Patrick Lewis reflects on the importance of reading classic literature such as *Alice in Wonderland* or *The Wind in the Willows*. He then contributes a classic humorous poem entitled, "Mosquito." Steven Kroll reports that he is not a poet, but is a writer who occasionally chooses to compose poetry. His brief account of coping in "When My Friends All Moved Away," provides encouragement and a smile for readers who have endured similar separation. Jim Daniels writes "Speech Class (for Joe)," revealing how his own struggle with speech therapy gave him greater sensitivity to others in his class. Gary Soto pays tribute to his baseball icon, Hector Moreno, in "Black Hair." Some other contributors include Nancy Willard, Cynthia Rylant, and Russell Hoban, all with impressive credentials in writing picture books for younger children as well as their poetic offerings. Of course, there is the expected roster listing Paul Fleischman, Jack Prelutsky, Myra Cohn Livingston, X.J. Kennedy, Eve Merriam, Karla Kuskin and Valerie Worth. Only the rich insights presented rival the variety of poetry by nearly forty authors. With an index of poets that reads more like a hall of fame for modern writers, this little collection, especially with its personal vignettes, is a treasure for those who write, read, or teach poetry or any variety of creative writing.

92   Janeczko, Paul B., comp., *Postcard Poems*, Bradbury Press, 1979 (hardcover), ISBN 0–87888–155–7, 105 pp., grades 9 and up.

It is almost a cliché to state that poetry is meant to be shared. However, in his collection of 104 poems, Paul Janeczko gives a fresh meaning to the thought. This sampling of more than seventy well-established writers brings together verses brief enough to write on a note card, send on a postcard, or memorize on a whim—not to mention post in a classroom. Janeczko's premise is that such literature is a gift best accepted and passed on from one recipient to the next, then to the next, and so on. Fourteen untitled chapters list from four to ten selections. "Gift," by Judith Hemschemeyer, is the opening piece and sets the mood for the entire work. In "Crows," by William Witherup, readers are given unique thoughts on socializing and sharing beverages. Valerie Worth brings new vision to a simple walk with "Daisies." Walt Whitman bids farewell with a tribute to the enduring quality of poetry with "No Labor-Saving Machine." Special features include an acknowledgments page, Janeczko's inviting introduction, and an index of poets. For those looking for a collection of verses that can be enjoyed in a few minutes each day, this is an ideal package.

93   Janeczko, Paul B., comp., *Preposterous: Poems of Youth*, Orchard Books, 1991 (hardcover), ISBN 0–531–05901–4, 134 pp., grades 10 and up.

Janceczko's anthology *Preposterous* purports to be a collection of "Poems of Youth." The promotional statement on the bookcover boasts a collection of 108 poems by 82 people who know the land. Just as the faces on the bookcover jacket indicate, however, many of these featured young adults appear to be fragmented, unhappy people. There is a heavy focus on negative experiences and behavior patterns. The only guide for the reader is an index of poets included at the back of the book. There is no subject designation given, but titles are roughly arranged by topics such as family issues, including sibling relationships, in "Rescue," parents in "Tableau," and grandparents in "Explaining." Also touched upon are peer relationships in "The Telling Tree," and death in "Anthony." Poems such as "Evening Dawn," a song of joy at nature's glorious sunset, and "Music Lessons," a child's first discovery of the beauty of musical expression, provide lighter moments. In spite of the heaviness of the subject matter, undoubtedly many teens would relate to one or more of the situations the poets themselves have encountered.

94 Janeczko, Paul B., *Stardust Hotel*, illus. by Dorothy Leech, Orchard Books, 1993 (hardcover), ISBN 0–531–05498–5, 64 pp., grades 10 and up.

In this volume, which targets the young adult audience, Leary, age fourteen, shares his impressions of the people who inhabit the Stardust Hotel, which his parents own. In free-verse poems he introduces the reader to his parents, former flower children who insist on his calling them Nick and Lucy, and friends like Becky Loudermilk, whose father beats her. Then there is Maisie Whitman, the lady barber who allows Leary to help her work on a prize '57 Chevy Impala in the evenings. Rusty Hughes is a former minor league baseball player who now works at the A&P. Not all of the characters presented in Janeczko's scrapbook are admirable, but the author reveals their strengths and shortcomings in a matter-of-fact tone of voice, expressing neither worship nor disdain. The mood of these poems varies from the innocent exuberance of "First Snow" to the grief surrounding the death of a loved one in "Nesterenko." Although the teacher may wish to exercise discretion in the presentation of these selections, the poems on the whole, are touching and insightful.

95 Janeczko, Paul B., comp., *Stone Bench in an Empty Park*, photo. by Henri Silberman, Orchard Books, 2000 (hardcover), ISBN 0–531–30259–8, unpaged, grades 6 and up.

Using the ancient Japanese form of poetry called haiku, the entries found in *Stone Bench in an Empty Park* encourage the reader to see the beauty found in the everyday. Although many anthologies exalt the glories of nature in the wild, this grouping cultivates an appreciation for urban living. Silberman's thought-provoking black and white photos are a major factor in the effectiveness of this work. Although his stated purpose is not to present literal interpretations of the poems, in most instances he comes very close. Contributors such as Jane Yolen, Myra Cohn Livingston, and Nikki Grimes will be names well known to those familiar with poetry for youth. In an introduction the compiler explains the poetical form of haiku as well as sets the tone for the book. A note from the photographer explains his approach and encourages readers to look below the surface to find the beauty around them.

96 Janeczko, Paul B., comp., *Strings: A Gathering of Family Poems*, Bradbury Press, 1984 (hardcover), ISBN 0–02–747790–8, 161 pp., grades 9 and up.

Poignant, powerful, and provocative is this collection designed by Paul Janeczko. Most certainly all readers who have families, as well as those who have lost them will find some selections that touch the heart. Janeczko has chosen well from the eighty-four poets represented to present a balanced view of this essential unit of life. The 128 poems are divided into topical chapters. In "From

Wives and Husbands," young adults may gain insight about their own parents from Gary Margolis' intimate portrait "On the Eve of Our Anniversary." "From Parents" enlightens the teen with a variety of adult observations, even on the adoption of a stray cat, "Murgatroyd," by Celeste Turner Wright. "From Children" boasts the greatest number of entries and encompasses every aspect of childhood from Sandra Hockman's unsuccessful efforts at communication with her father in "Clay and Water" to David Huddle's loving tribute to his dad "In White Tie." Any remaining family members are represented in chapters entitled "From Brothers and Sisters," "From Cousins," "From Nieces and Nephews," and "From Grandchildren." Each piece shares a voice and view that will connect with some reader.

Although most selections are written from the adult perspective, young readers are given glimpses into generation gaps, wistful wishes, and explanation of emotions that open the door to insight and understanding in tenuous and troubled relationships. For those who enjoy the security of stable families, many verses will pleasantly reflect what they already enjoy. Janeczko closes with an extensive acknowledgments section and an index of poets.

97 Janeczko, Paul B., *That Sweet Diamond: Baseball Poems*, illus. by Carole Katchen, Atheneum Books for Young Readers, 1998 (hardcover), ISBN 0–689–80735–X, unpaged, grades 7 and up.

Although the format of this collection may seem to be that of a children's picture book, the verses included cross all age levels. The one-to-one match of illustration and text gives readers the illusion of being on the scene. Carole Katchen's hazy pastels lend the shimmer of summer heat to each spread. Within the scope of the nineteen poems, Janeczko writes about all aspects of the game. He introduces the collection with "Before the Game" and concludes with "After the Game." In between are portrayed players, spectators, and vendors. The aches and pains of the man behind the plate are bemoaned in "Catcher Sings the Blues." Blessings are implored for the most controversial participant in "Prayer for the Umpire." Age-old talents are unveiled in "How to Spit." Special encouragement offered by spectators is celebrated in "Nuns." What a marvelous tribute to the people who make the sport "sweet." Teachers will find this simple collection especially encouraging in spring when thoughts turn to baseball. Creative writing, collages, music, legends, newspaper clippings could all embellish this delightful anthology.

98 Janeczko, Paul B., comp., *Very Best (Almost) Friends: Poems of Friendship*, illus. by Christine Davenier, Candlewick Press, 1999 (hardcover), ISBN 0–7636–0475–5, 87 pp., grades 6 and up.

The expression of friendship knows no age, gender, or ethnic boundaries. Paul Janeczko has searched out and compiled twenty-four verses that address this many-faceted phenomenon that is almost impossible to adequately express on paper. The contemporary poets who speak in this pocket-sized anthology cover the fragile relationship from every angle. Jim Daniels, in "Blubber Lips," tells how sometimes empathy results in an unforgettable lesson. Charlotte Zolotow celebrates the unbridled joy of having a special friend in "People." Karla Kuskin acknowledges the courage bestowed by friendship in "To You." All is not sweetness and light, however, as X.J. Kennedy emphatically states in "My Stupid Parakeet Named after You" and John Ciardi sarcastically quips in "Who?" Christine Davenier's lively illustrations brighten each page and are perfectly paired with the verses in this little treasure. Concluding permission pages offer further resources from each contributor.

99 Janeczko, Paul B., comp., *Wherever Home Begins*, Orchard Books, 1995 (hardcover), ISBN 0–531–09481–2, 114 pp., grades 10 and up.

Place often defines a person to the world, as well as to the individual himself. In this collection, poems are grouped by their location and accompanying ambiance. More than seventy-five writers contribute the one hundred verses that visit a wide variety of places from caves and prairies to diners and bars. Eighteen untitled chapters include verses numbering from one to fourteen loosely based on some uniting feature of geography. The young adult audience will know most of the contributors. Each seems to be writing out of deep emotional attachment to the setting or experience related to a memorable event. Jim Wayne Miller expresses feelings of grief in "Closing the House." In contrast, Gary Soto pictures life on a street that he treasures in "Street." Judith Hemschemeyer catches childhood responses to sitting in the backseat of her family car in "The Ride Home." Jonathan Holden captures that excited security of approaching the old familiar house in "Home." The chief impact of the collection may be the desire that arises in the reader to capture in verse some place of solitude or activity that triggers significant memories. To spark such a response would make the anthology of even greater value. Janeczko concludes his collection with an acknowledgments page and a combined index of poets and titles.

100 Jin, Ha, *Between Silences: A Voice from China*, University of Chicago Press, 1990 (hardcover), ISBN 0–226–39987–7, 79 pp., grades 10 and up.

In this slim anthology, Ha Jin has given expression to the thoughts and feelings of the people of China who lived through the Cultural Revolution. His focus is not on the events of history, but the people who were shaped by these experiences. They are not presented only as victims, however, but as participants and shapers of this history. "Towards a Battlefield" focuses on the poet's experiences as a soldier on the Russian border. Although soldiers of any war could identify with the emotions behind many of these titles, "A Hero's Mother Blames Her Daughter" highlights the importance of family honor in the Chinese culture. With devastating understatement, the poems of chapter two, such as "The Dissolution of a Kingdom," reveal the moral price tag of the Revolution. In chapter three, "No Tears for Love" tells of loves lost, but not forgotten. "A Young Worker's Lament to His Former Girlfriend" demonstrates the cooling effect political indoctrination can have on passion. "An Old Red Guard's Reply" indicates the thrust of the poems in chapter four, titled "Ways." It describes how the deceptions of the Revolution have caused people to despair of ever knowing the truth and have led them to blindly accept what they are told. A preface explains the author's approach to his writing, and a table of contents gives the only direction to the body of the work.

101 Johnson, Dave, ed., *Movin': Teen Poets Take Voice*, illus. by Chris Raschka, Orchard Books, 2000 (hardcover), ISBN 0–531–30258–X, grades 8 and up.

Movin' was created by a cooperative effort between Poets House and The New York Public Library. Designing a program called Poetry-in-the-Branches, these groups combined readings, writing workshops, and discussions for adults and young adults. The poetry included in this volume was the end product of these workshops. Poems were also submitted through Wordsmiths, a part of *TeenLink*, The New York Public Library's young adult web site (*http://www.nypl.org/branch/teen*). Whether giving voice to dreams as in "Ice-skating Dreams," speaking of family as in "If I Could Give Back," or sharing memories from the past in "Boy on a Tricycle," participants drew inspiration from every-day life and shared a desire to give voice to their thoughts. "Music" appears both in English and Spanish versions. Sparse black and white drawings by Chris Raschka provide an effective accent to the verse. There is no index and there are no extra helps to guide the reader. The success of this volume has given legitimacy to the creative efforts of all involved and may inspire young people not only to enjoy the art form but to believe that they too can express themselves in verse.

102 Johnson, James Weldon, *Lift Every Voice and Sing*, illus. by Elizabeth Catlett, Walker and Company, 1993 (hardcover), ISBN 0–8027–8250–7, unpaged, grades 6 and up.

Written for school children in 1900, James Weldon Johnson's *Lift Every Voice and Sing* has become known as the African American national anthem. Set to music by his brother J. Rosamond, these lyrics acknowledge evil suffered but encourage the soul to freedom, hope, and strength for battles yet to come. The twelve linocut illustrations, done in colored pencil, gouache, and water colors, portray the life of blacks in Africa, under the burden of slavery, and in modern times. These strong lined prints were created independently, then brought together with Johnson's verse to create this special volume in picture-book format. The music and words in manuscript form are found at the back of the book along with the original captions given to Catlett's works of art. A lengthy introduction by Jim Haskins gives helpful background information about the author and the illustrator.

103 Johnston, Patricia Irwin, comp., *Perspectives on a Grafted Tree*, illus. by Diana L. Stanley, Perspectives Press, 1983 (hardcover), ISBN 0–9609504–0–0, 144 pp., grades 6 and up.

With the increase of teenage pregnancies, Patricia Johnson's collection of poems about adoption may find a ready audience among young adults. Selections are written from the perspective of a mother giving up a child for adoption as in "Confession" and a would-be parent yearning to fill empty arms with another's child as in "On the Night of Andrew's Birth." The thoughts of adopted children wondering about their unknown heritage are found in "Bloodlines," "Mother May I," and "The Chosen One." Since most of these poems are contributed by nonprofessional writers, there is a noticeable fluctuation in the quality of verse. Although drawn by the same artist, the black and white illustrations also vary greatly in quality. Those struggling with the issues in question, however, should be able to find in one or more of the selections an expression for the grief, the fears, the hopes and the joys they have experienced. A bibliography of reading and resources offers additional titles of interest to those involved in adoption. Since few of the poets are well known, the author index provided will be less helpful than the four-page table of contents. A lengthy introduction discusses adoption issues from all sides and effectively sets the stage for the poems to follow.

104 Kilcher, Jewel, *A Night Without Armor: Poems*, Scholastic, 1998 (paperback), ISBN 0–439–10988–4, 63 pp., grades 9 and up.

Speaking from her own childhood and adolescent experiences, Jewel Kilcher uses verse to tell of both the good times and the bad times of her life. Her struggles to establish an identity are expressed in "Pretty" and "I Am Not from Here." The loneliness of her life on the road finds release in "The Strip 1," "The Strip 2," and "Road Spent." The effects of her parents' divorce surface in "After the Divorce." In spite of her youth, Kilcher demonstrates maturity of thought and a great ability to use the art form of poetry. This edition by Scholastic seems to be excerpted from the original HarperCollins publication, omitting some of the more evocative pieces. There is no index and there does not seem to be any special order to the poems. Young people's familiarity with the author's music should encourage them to try her poetry. There is reason to believe that as they read these verses, young people will not only hear their own thoughts couched in another's words, but will be inspired to find release for their ideas and feelings through poetry of their own composition.

105 Knudson, R. Rozanne, and May Swenson, eds., *American Sports Poems*, Orchard Books, 1989 (hardcover), ISBN 0–531–05753–4, 226 pp., grades 6 and up.

Grouping their selections by type of activity, Knudson and Swenson have provided verses to please every kind of sports participant or sports fan. Individual pastimes of surfing, hunting, swimming, tennis, and running find their place with the team efforts of baseball, basketball, football, hockey, volleyball and other athletic endeavors. Even skydiving and bronco riding are included. Athletic heroes such as Babe Ruth, Wilt Chamberlain, and Jackie Robinson are eulogized in poems ranging from two lines to two pages in length. Works by Walt Whitman, Carl Sandburg, Robert Frost, Ogden Nash, and John Updike are printed next to those of more contemporary and lesser-known poets. The broad array of over twenty-five sports and the variety of poetic styles represented in these 155 titles should provide something to please every teen. Author, title, and subject indexes provide easy access. Enlightening notes about featured players and various poets are contained in "Among the Poets and Players." The names of players are noted in their order of appearance in the volume.

106 Koch, Kenneth, and Kate Farrell, eds., *Sleeping on the Wing: An Anthology of Modern Poetry with Essays on Reading and Writing*, Vintage Books, 1981 (paperback), ISBN 0–394–74364–4, 313 pp., grades 8 and up.

To those who readily recognize the names of the compilers of this collection, there is a foreshadowing of practicality, creativity, and wisdom in the aesthetic experience about to take place. To read the lengthy and user-friendly introduction, in which the editors explain the rationale for their choice of poets, is to be assured that one has chosen well to spend his/her time between the covers of this work.

Award-winning writer Kenneth Koch, who is paired here with fellow teacher Kate Farrell, takes up the cause of enjoying poetry through reading and writing with the zeal of an evangelist preaching to a world that is slipping into oblivion. His enthusiasm for the medium is contagious both among general readers and his students. Speaking from years of teaching in both high school and college, Koch invites the reader to write and insists that both processes are mutually enhancing. At the very outset of this collection, the teacher in Koch is evident.

His introduction is directed to students and is written in a first-person style that lends an air of intimacy in communication between editor and reader. He acts as a sort of public relations agent for poetry in general, by encouraging students to see the creative, adventurous aspect to writing, as he attempts to dispel fears of putting feelings on paper.

Following the introduction are twenty-three divisions, titled by the name of the contributing poet. Koch and Farrell have selected contemporary poets from the mid-nineteenth century to the time of publication. Most are English; others represent Spain, Germany, France, and Russia. In theme and expression, there is universal appeal. Poems introduce each section. Pieces vary in length from a few lines as in "Alba" by Ezra Pound, to many pages in "Song of Myself," by Walt Whitman. Some themes included are nature, death, rural and urban life, faith, and observations on life. Contributors vary in tone from the praise poems of Gerard Manley Hopkins, a Jesuit priest, to the sad/angry questioning of Leroi Jones (Imamu Amiri Bakara) who embraces Islam. The editors conclude with a note to teachers in which they state that the book was compiled with the plan that it be used as a textbook and therefore composition and content are student directed. However, useful suggestions to the teacher are also included. Brief biographical sketches of the contributors complete this useful volume.

107 Lamb, Walter, ed., *Always Begin Where You Are: Themes in Poetry and Song*, McGraw-Hill, 1979 (hardcover), ISBN 0–07–035921–0, 276 pp., grades 9 and up.

Believing that most teens have dismissed poetry because they have been exposed to dull, ambiguous selections that seem to have no relation to their lives, Lamb has compiled an anthology of verse with subjects that directly concern young people today. Chapter headings read like an adolescent psychology text: "Parents and Their Children"; "Identity: Defining Yourself"; "Male/Female"; "Individuals and Oddballs"; "Our Many Moods"; and "Success: What Is It?". "Looking for America," the last chapter, includes works that treat the multicultural makeup of our nation.

Lamb includes works as diverse as those from the classic poets Alexander Pope, Robert Frost, and Carl Sandburg, to lyrics from songwriters Willie Nelson, Joni Mitchell, and Harry Chapin. Included among the poems that celebrate the family are "The Young Girl's Song," and "Held Back." These works echo the feelings of youth, while the voice and opinions of parents are expressed in "A Father Sees a Son Nearing Manhood." Many titles speak of feelings universal to all ages, such as loneliness, fear, grief, or hope. Some poems express problems unique to those whose lives are filled with special needs, such as "Blind Man" and "Freak Show," or address the experiences of various cultures adjusting to this country in "The Tropics in New York," "Soul," and "Keeping Hair."

Unique to this book is the extensive section of "Author's Notes to the Reader" in which Lamb defines poetry and extols its benefits to the student. His chapter introductions not only set the stage for the poems that follow, but give specific insight to each title. A vocabulary check appears at the beginning of each cluster to define words that may not be familiar to the reader. These teaching aids, coupled with the appropriateness of the selection, make this an anthology of great usefulness in the classroom.

108 L'Amour, Louis, *Smoke from This Altar*, Bantam Books, 1990 (hardcover), ISBN 0–553–07349–4, 75 pp., grades 10 and up.

For most readers, poetry is not the genre that readily springs to mind at the name of Louis L'Amour. Best known for his action packed Western novels, L'Amour has been one of the most popular and prolific writers of American novels in this century, doubtless, the most popular of his genre. In the introduction, Kathy L'Amour, wife of the author, shares interesting glimpses into the life of her renowned husband. She reveals the role poetry played in his life, as well as the significance of this particular collection in their relationship. It is somewhat amazing to read that this little volume assisted in launching his career as a writer.

In this anthology are a number of his previously published poems, but some new ones as well. His themes are as varied as lost love in "Nocturne," contentment in "Let it Snow," and literary humor in "I Haven't Read Gone With the Wind." For those who are already avid readers of L'Amour's novels, this small book will simply enlarge their admiration for the talented author. For those just being initiated into his work, this collection introduces a sensitive, insightful writer.

109 Larrick, Nancy, ed., *Bring Me All Your Dreams*, photo. by Larry Mulvehill, M. Evans and Company, 1980 (paperback), ISBN 0–87131–550–5, 110 pp., grades 6–12.

From childhood wishes to the poems of tribal groups such as "The Song of a Drum," Nancy Larrick's collection includes poems about all types of dreams. Dreams of equality find voice in "Keep to the March." Dreams of accomplishment flow out of "I, Icarus." John Ciardi imagines the dreams of animals and inanimate objects in "The Army Horse and the Army Jeep." Even that soft, undefined time between waking and sleeping is given words in "Lullaby." Choices are divided into six sections titled: "I Dream and I Dream"; "When I Was But a Child, I Dreamed a Wondrous Dream"; "It was More Fun When I Dreamed High"; "Gather Out of Stardust . . . One Handful of Dream Dust"; "The Wind Sings Songs of Far Away"; and "Hold Fast to Dreams." Titles can be found through the table of contents, index of first lines, and index to poems and poets. Helpful biographical information about the poets included in the anthology fills seven pages.

110 Larrick, Nancy, comp., *Crazy To Be Alive in Such a Strange World: Poems About People*, photo. by Alexander L. Crosby, M. Evans and Company, 1977 (paperback), ISBN 0–87131–566–1, 171 pp., grades 6 and up.

Larrick enlisted the help of young people in choosing which titles would be included in *Crazy to be Alive in Such a Strange World*. Well-known poets such as Carl Sandburg, William Carlos Williams, and Langston Hughes find a place here along with modern writers Nikki Giovanni, Shel Silverstein, and newer, lesser-known writers. As is common with Larrick's collections, all selections use language young people know and understand. The clothing dates a few of the photos, but taken as a whole, these pictures, shot in the United States, England, France, Mexico, Peru, and East Africa, form a timeless tapestry of unforgettable faces.

Headings for the nine chapter divisions are taken from the first lines of poems. Grouped by topics like childhood, family, adolescence, love, work, and aging, they build in impact to create a sense of community as expressed in the headings "On This Street We Two Pass" and "I Sit and Look Out on the Sorrows of the World." The poems themselves are a study in contrasts with the kindness in "Elegy" standing opposite the cruelty in "For Laurence Jones." The inner city reality of "Feeding the Lions" is distinct from the rural experience of "Hay for the Horses." And the solitude of old age in "Loneliness" differs sharply with the unfettered joy of childhood in "Laughing Child." A seventeen-page "Meet the Poets" section gives broad introduction to the background of contributors. Table of contents, index of poets and titles, and an index of first lines complete the guidance given to the reader.

111 Larrick, Nancy, comp., *On City Streets*, photo. by David Sagarin, M. Evans and Company, 1968 (paperback), ISBN 0–87131–551–3, 158 pp., grades 6 and up.

Believing that most anthologies for young people concentrate on the virtues of rural life, while the majority of youth live in an urban setting, Nancy Larrick has created a volume of verse designed to extol the vibrancy of city life. To determine which titles to include in her collection, the compiler ventured into school systems and allowed young people to do the choosing. The final selection of poems was the favorites of suburban as well as inner-city youth. Photo illustrations add a reality to those reflections that could not be matched by drawings. Although cars and clothing date a few of the photos, the mood and feel effectively come through. Helps for the reader include an index of poets and titles, a separate index of first lines, and a profile of the compiler. The titles are arranged by the general chapter headings of "Sounds," "People in the City," "Housing," "Children," "Parks," and "The Night." Some speak of loneliness or grief, such as "A Sad Song about Greenwich Village" and "Could be." Humor is injected with "Alligator on the Escalator," a nonsense poem. Most simply record the ebb and flow of everyday life in the city.

112 Larrick, Nancy, ed., *Piping Down the Valleys Wild*, Dell Publishing Company, 1968 (paperback), ISBN 0–440–46952–X, 247 pp., grades 6 and up.

Nancy Larrick provides an introduction to poets such as John Masefield, Edward Lear, Carl Sandburg, John Ciardi, and others of equal reputation in their least complex and arguably their most enjoyable works in this long popular anthology. Although this collection is generally considered to be for children, there are a number of selections included that are classics and will find a home in the heart of the young adult. Their feelings are mirrored in a number of pieces. Frustration with peers may find an apt metaphor in Walt Whitman's "I Think I Could Turn and Live with Animals." Companionship and pleasure in simple things is demonstrated in Robert Frost's "The Pasture." Joy in nature is expressed in Langston Hughes' "April Rain Song." The young person who occasionally prefers the peace of solitude will identify with "Afternoon on a Hill" by Edna St. Vincent Millay.

The collection lists over one hundred authors with selections for an audience of children, young adults and adults. Topics are divided into sixteen chapters with intriguing titles such as "The city spreads its wings . . . ," "I was one of the children told . . . ," and "A dozen dreams to dance to you. . . ." each lifted from a line in a poem found in that section. Special features include an index of authors and titles, an index of first lines, and an acknowledgments page.

113 Larrick, Nancy, comp., *Room for Me and a Mountain Lion*, M. Evans and Company, 1974 (paperback), ISBN 0–87131–569–6, 191 pp., grades 6 and up.

The call of the wilderness, the need for open space, and a deep appreciation for nature are the motivating themes behind these poems collected by Nancy Larrick. Pieces like "Mountain Lion" and "Requiem for a River" convey deep sorrow over man's abusive disregard of our earth's resources. Others, such as "Reading in the Rain," record a simple satisfaction in being a part of this world. Various natural areas and weather conditions are highlighted by chapter divisions including mountains, woods, prairies, bodies of water, ice and snow, and open fields. This anthology would be an excellent resource for cross-curriculum study in science and history. Varying in length, the poems are easily understood and appeal to a wide variety of reading levels. They are illustrated with black and white photographs of great beauty. Indexes are provided to first lines and to poems and poets. The compiler's introduction outlines the wilderness experiences that provided the impetus for this collection.

114 Lee, Francis, ed., *When the Rain Sings: Poems by Young Native Americans*, Simon and Schuster Books for Young Readers, 1999 (hardcover), ISBN 0–689–82283–9, 74 pp., grades 6 and up.

Inspired by the mentoring program Wordcraft Circle of Native Writers and Storytellers, Lee and others conceived the brainchild that led to this collection. Pictures of objects and archival photographs from the Smithsonian Institution's National Museum of the American Indian were sent out to students in Indian schools across the country. The young people were asked to respond in writing, especially to those artifacts representing their culture group. This small anthology is the result.

Photographs and text are paired on adjacent pages. Name, age, grade, school, tribe, city, and state identify writers. Students ranging in age from seven to seventeen penned the thirty-seven poems. A foreword by W. Richard West paying tribute to the insight and artistry of the youthful authors precedes the text of the book. Elizabeth Woody of the Confederated Tribes of the Warm Spring Reservation contributes an introduction. West concludes the introductory material with an acknowledgments page. Chapter headings are identified by the following tribes: Ojibwe, Kiowa, Tohono O'odham (also including Yaqui and Pima), Hopi, and Ute. Themes of the verses vary from the esoteric focus of reservation life to universal subjects such as freedom, nature, and family life. Concluding pages list a brief synopsis of each Indian Nation represented, information about the artifacts in the illustrations, and photo credits.

115 Levin, Jonathan, ed., *Poetry for Young People: Walt Whitman*, illus. by Jim Burke, Sterling Publishing Company, 1997 (hardcover), ISBN 0–8069–9530–0, 48 pp., grades 6 and up.

In this collection of more than twenty-five poems and excerpts from longer poems, Jim Burke provides illustrations that have an earthy feel matching the tone of Whitman's poetry. A biographical introduction written by the editor gives a background to understanding the poet. Difficult words with their definitions are listed at the bottom of each page. An index gives an alphabetical guide to the poems included. Whitman does not shy away from unpleasant subjects such as slavery in "A Man's Body at Auction" and war and death in "The Artilleryman's Vision." He shows a great respect and appreciation for nature in "Miracles" and a love of the strength and diversity of America in "I Hear America Singing." Whitman's poetry exudes an energy and passion that should appeal to the adolescent. Teens may also be able to identify with his voyage of self-discovery in "I Tramp a Perpetual Journey" (taken from *Song of Myself*).

116 Lewis, J. Patrick, *Black Swan, White Crow*, illus. by Chris Manson, Atheneum Books for Young Readers (hardcover), 1995, ISBN 0–689–31899–5, unpaged, grades 5–10.

This anthology features thirteen poems set on the left-hand page with striking, colored woodcut prints on the right. The subjects range from fish, to buffalo, to cornfields, but all selections give the readers a heightened appreciation for the world around them. In his introduction Lewis explains the standard form for haiku and encourages young people to try writing it themselves. This volume makes a good show-and-tell example of artistic expression for students to follow.

117 Livingston, Myra Cohn, comp., *Call Down the Moon: Poems of Music*, Margaret K. McElderry Books, 1995 (hardcover), ISBN 0–689–80416–4, 170 pp., grades 6 and up.

Livingston has collected into one volume over one hundred poems that relate to music. Whether eulogizing musical heroes in "Ray Charles," and "On Rachmaninoff's Birthday," or acknowledging the songs of nature in "Rain," and from "Chamber Music I," these chosen titles celebrate the magic of musical expression. "Blues," in "So You Want to Hear the Blues," finds a place of acceptance next to Brahms, honored in "Behind the Beard."

Divided into twelve sections, chapters carry the names of types of instruments including keyboards and strings, brass and percussion, and woodwinds. Other parts cover singers, time to practice, and music in the air. The reader is further guided by indexes to authors, titles, first lines and translators. Translated works from French, Latin, Spanish, Chinese, and Japanese emphasize the universality of this form of communication, which touches all cultures and ways of life. Classic authors such as Samuel Coleridge and Alfred Lord Tennyson are side-by-side with the American poets, Walt Whitman, X.J. Kennedy, and Edward Lear. Traditional spirituals and humorous limericks round out the selections.

118 Livingston, Myra Cohn, comp., *Christmas Poems*, illus. by Trina Schart Hyman, Holiday House, 1984 (hardcover), ISBN 0–8234–0508–7, 32 pp., grades 6 and up.

Although the illustrations in this collection seem designed with the younger reader in mind, the verses selected are as ageless as Christmas. Award-winning artist Trina Schart Hyman sets the scene with her signature characters peering out of each page and inviting the reader in. Myra Cohn Livingston has chosen to highlight a cross-section of the winter holiday from the traditional Christmas story of the Bible to contemporary writers. In "Kaleidoscope" X.J. Kennedy combines carols, candy canes, and other symbols of Christmas in picturesque descriptions of both stable and village streets. Christina Rossetti poses the unanswerable question, "What Can I Give Him?" David McCord offers sobering thoughts of world-wide concern for peace in "Christmas Prayer." The eighteen poems, illustrated in green, red, and brown, combine in a nice package to share at a universally special time of the year. A table of contents and acknowledgments page offer helpful information to complete the collection.

119 Livingston, Myra Cohn, *Cricket Never Does: A Collection of Haiku and Tanka*, illus. by Kees de Kiefte, Margaret K. McElderry Books, 1997 (hardcover), ISBN 0–689–81123–3, 42 pp., grades 6 and up.

Livingston has borrowed from the Japanese forms of haiku and tanka to create sixty-seven selections to entice the reader. Each season of the year is given its own section introduced by the spare black and white sketches of Kees de Kiefte. The ocean, weather, flowers, birds, and other aspects of nature are awarded a place of honor in verse. The quality of the poet's work sets a high standard for young people to emulate.

120 Livingston, Myra Cohn, ed., *Easter Poems*, illus. by John Wallner, Holiday House, 1985 (hardcover), ISBN 0–8234–0546–X, 32 pp., grades 6 and up.

Myra Cohn Livingston offers a small basket of verses in tribute to the Christian celebration of the Resurrection. She has selected some traditional poems, included translations from Russia and Germany, and commissioned others specifically for this collection. John Wallner's ethereal pen and ink drawings add their own mystical tone to the work. A list of contributors reads like a roll call in the poet's hall of fame. Joan Aiken writes wistfully in "Kyrie Eleison" of her desire for peace. X.J. Kennedy draws a parallel between the familiar egg, a tulip bulb, and the empty tomb in "These Three." Emanuel Di Pasquale explores cultural celebrations in "Sicilian Easter Sunday." David McCord pens a verse of praise and gratitude in an excerpt from "Easter Morning." On the acknowledgments page Livingston recognizes the poets who wrote specifically for this anthology. She also lists poems and resources for the four pieces that were already in print.

121 Livingston, Myra Cohn, ed., *I Like You If You Like Me*, Margaret K. McElderry Books, 1987 (hardcover), ISBN 0–689–50408–X, 144 pp., grades 5 and up.

The selection in Livingston's collection is eclectic, with ninety titles included by authors from eighth-century China to twentieth-century America. They vary from light verse that might be found in an autograph album to serious poetry for the adult. The nonsense lines of Edward Lear contrast with the serious lines of Langston Hughes and Carl Sandburg. The titles of the nine divisions of the book reflect a diversity of experiences regarding friendship. From "Lonesome All Alone" to "We're Going to Be Good Friends," times of melancholy as well as joyous celebration find expression. Even animals are included in the division titled "The Friendly Beasts." Most selections are short, with the exception of "The Owl's Bedtime Story" by Randall Jarrell. With such variety, this volume will appeal to a large age range. Indexes to titles, first lines, authors and translators expand access.

122 Livingston, Myra Cohn, comp, *If the Owl Calls Again: A Collection of Owl Poems*, illus. by Antonio Frasconi, Margaret K. McElderry Books, 1990 (hardcover), ISBN 0–68950–501–9, 114 pp., grades 6 and up.

Mysterious and nocturnal, the owl has provided inspiration for a wide variety of verses. This anthology catalogs the thoughts of sixty-two poets as they ponder this unique creature. In her introduction, Livingston addresses the mystique accompanying the look, the sound, and the flight of this solemn-eyed bird. Divided into five chapters of about twenty pages each, this collection offers verses on owls in the light, in flight, of delight, of night and those that may cause fright. Charles Causley's humorous verse, "The Owl Looked out of the Ivy Bush" poses the problem faced by the bird that uttered the reverse of what was expected. John Haines voices his desire to fly with the elusive avian in the title poem, "If the Owl Calls Again." Leonard Clark takes an opposing and negative view of the winged creature in "Owls." Whatever the reader's sentiments regarding the mystical bird, a corresponding verse may be found in this collection of nearly eighty poems. To assist the reader in finding the desired piece, there are indexes of authors, translators, titles, and first lines.

123 Livingston, Myra Cohn, *Monkey Puzzle and Other Poems*, illus. by Antonio Frasconi, Atheneum, 1984 (hardcover), ISBN 0–689–50310–5, 54 pp., grades 6 and up.

After observing the beauty of trees of every size and description, Livingston shares the special characteristics of each with her readers. From the unusual monkey puzzle tree in the title poem to the common maple, varieties are chosen from all parts of the country. The shapes of the mimosa, douglas fir, and the cypress are represented by the arrangement of the words on the page. Varying in length from the three-line tribute to the jacaranda and bristlecone pine to the four-page tribute to the threatened rainforests of Papua, New Guinea, most of Livingston's poems are short and vibrantly descriptive. Frasconi's woodcut illustrations support the mood and message of the verse. This would be an excellent tie-in to science units on plants.

124 Livingston, Myra Cohn, *Sky Songs*, illus. by Leonard Everett Fisher, Holiday House, 1984 (hardcover), ISBN 0–8234–0502–8, 31 pp., grades 7 and up.

For all those who have gazed at the sky in wonder, this collection provides a tantalizing feast for the mind and the eye. All fourteen poems have celestial bodies as their subjects. The dazzling illustrations were created in acrylic on textured paper in the same size as they appear in the book and then transferred by laser light scanning. The result is stunning. Together, text and illustration form a seamless composition. Self-explanatory and simple titles belie the beauty of thought and language in the free verse compositions. "Stars" captures something of the infinite number of these points of light. "Morning Sky" compares the fresh beauty of sunrise to an astrodome where games are about to begin. "Snow" likens the wintry powder to sheets, a comforter, and a sleeping bag made of snowflakes. Finally, "Sunset" portrays the day elegantly dressed for dinner. Taken altogether, this collection is an impressive blend of written and visual art.

125 Livingston, Myra Cohn, comp., *Thanksgiving Poems*, illus. by Stephen Gammell, Holiday House, 1985 (hardcover), ISBN 0–8234–0570–2, 30 pp., grades 7 and up.

A picture book, a collection of grateful thoughts, an anthology of praise across centuries and cultures would all serve as descriptors for this perfectly matched volume of art and verse. Livingston and Gammell have created a small masterpiece in recognition of the holiday that introduces the American season of celebration. Selections include works by contemporary and traditional writers, Native Americans and "more newly Americans." Topics range from humor to sacred worship. X.J. Kennedy paints a realistic portrait of feeling and food in "Family Reunion." Felice Holman shares philosophical thoughts from the turkey that was too skinny to be eaten in "Gobbeldy-Gobble." Emanuel Di Pasquale celebrates the discovery of a free land in "Joy of an Immigrant, a Thanksgiving." There are also selections that commemorate planting and harvest—from "Songs in the Garden of the House God" (Navajo), and "Song of the Osage Woman" (Osage). Although the format is that of a picture book for elementary school children, the illustrations are appropriate for all ages, as is the content of the poems. An acknowledgments page lists resources at the conclusion of the text.

126 Livingston, Myra Cohn, ed., *A Time to Talk: Poems of Friendship*, Margaret K. McElderry Books, 1992 (hardcover), ISBN 0–689–50558–2, 115 pp., grades 9 and up.

Friendship is the theme of this collection. Myra Cohn Livingston, herself an accomplished writer, has blended her talents with more than sixty other authors to reveal in verse the changing face of a friend. Contributors range in chronology from Euripides to Paul Janeczko. Translations from Pablo Neruda, Bertolt Brecht, Liu Yu-his, Princess Diahaku, and others remind readers that concerns about companionship are universal. The text is divided into five chapters. Chapter 1, entitled "Friends," includes the title piece by Robert Frost. Chapter 2, "Friends in Company," concerns the social nature of being together, as in "A Revel" by Donagh MacDonagh. Chapter 3 addresses harsh reality in "Strange Friends, False Friends" with such verses as Lillian Morrison's "The Maze." Chapter 4 expresses the grief of lost friends as shared in "One Parting" by Carl Sandburg. Appropriately, chapter 5 is entitled "Friends Remembered" and reflects on both loss and sweet memories in works such as "Remember" by Christina Rossetti. Special features include an acknowledgments page, an index of authors, an index of titles, an index of first lines, and an index of translators. Although this anthology was not compiled specifically for the young adult audience, its focus on friendship gained, enjoyed, and lost will surely resonate with adolescent readers. It will serve as a source of inspiration for collections of similar verses or as a spark for creative writing.

127 Locker, Thomas, ed., *Home: A Journey Through America*, illus. by Thomas Locker, Harcourt Brace Jovanovich, 1998 (hardcover), ISBN 0–15–201473–X, unpaged, grades 6–9.

The American landscape is featured in this lovely book with poetry, prose, and the luminous oil paintings of Thomas Locker. Poems or excerpts from longer poetry or prose selections are framed with a border of twigs on the left-hand pages. A sentence or two of biographical information follows each author's contribution. Locker's rich and romantic landscapes fill the leaves on the right. Robert Frost begins the collection with an excerpt from "Once by the Pacific." A section from Henry David Thoreau's "Journal" brings it to rest in Concord, Massachusetts. Other authors familiar to the majority of readers are Carl Sandburg, Jane Yolen, Joseph Bruchac, and Willa Cather.

An introduction by Locker expresses his desire to portray the beauty and variety of the places Americans call home. A double-page map at the back of the book indicates the location honored by each author's title. This volume would be excellent to use in conjunction with Lee Bennett Hopkins' *My America* and Neil Philip's *Singing America* to enrich the study of this country's history and geography. It also would be a valuable resource to teach art appreciation.

128 Lyne, Sandford, comp., *Ten-Second Rainshowers: Poems by Young People*, illus. by Virginia Halstead, Simon and Schuster Books for Young Readers, 1996 (hardcover), ISBN 0–689–80113–0, 124 pp., grades 6–10.

As a participant in the Kennedy Center's Arts-in-Education program from 1983 to 1994, Sandford Lyne presented workshops on poetry writing to over 27,000 students in grades three through twelve. The gleanings of these years are found in *Ten-Second Rainshowers*. Selections by 130 poets are divided into six sections titled: "Angels in Bloom," "My Place," "Black and Blue," "Holding Hands," and "The Secret Kingdom." Coming from a diversity of socio-economic and ethnic backgrounds, young authors write of a variety of issues with simplicity and an open honesty. Feelings of self-doubt surface in "I Am an Ugly Girl," while "My Comfort" voices the poet's confidence and acceptance of self. "Rainshowers," the title poem, displays a spare eloquence in describing the natural world. Young people write with unsophisticated wisdom of relationships with parents and grandparents in "Warmth" and "Grandfather." Somewhat abstract, brightly colored illustrations divide the chapters.

129 Marcus, Leonard S., comp., *Lifelines: A Poetry Anthology Patterned on the Stages of Life*, Dutton Children's Books, 1994 (hardcover), ISBN 0–525–45164–1, 116 pp., grades 8 and up.

To many young adults, all that is important in life is "now," the immediate, the thing that is affecting them at the moment. Leonard Marcus brings together a collection of verses that depicts the stages of the human existence from birth to death and clearly demonstrates the importance and excitement of each era. Drawing from international poets, he presents views and experiences that are ethnically, economically, and emotionally diverse. Burma, China, England, Ireland, Israel, India, Iran (formerly Persia), Russia, and Romania are represented by writers from the eighth century to the present. An extensive biographical section informs readers about the life of contributors.

Chapter headings offer clues to the stages of life covered. Chapter 1, "Small Traveller," speaks of both the joy and pain of infancy and early childhood. E.B. White revels in the potential resting in a newborn in "Conch," James Wright ponders another side of potential in "Mutterings Over the Crib of a Deaf Child." Chapter 2, "I Am Old Enough," includes verses by young adults. John Logan paints a picture of brothers supporting one another in "The Brothers: Two Saltimbanques"; Gwendolyn Brooks reveals the destructive force of peer pressure in "We Real Cool." Chapter 3, "On Such a Hill," reveals the trials and joys of adulthood. Ogden Nash makes a wry observation on the purpose of adults in "The Parent," and Frank O'Hara emphatically reminds mothers of their responsibilities in "Ave Maria." Chapter 5, "In the End We Are All Light," looks at the twilight years with tenderness and humor. The title work by Liz Rosenberg attributes an encouraging double meaning to "light," and Maya Angelou puts her own special brand of humor into "On Aging." Taken altogether, this collection accomplishes just what Leonard Marcus intended; it causes the reader to value each moment in life as unique. Special features include the introduction, brief annotations on the contributors, an acknowledgments page, and a single index.

130 McCullough, Frances, comp., *Love Is Like the Lion's Tooth*. Harper and Row, 1984 (hardcover), ISBN 0–06–024138–1, 80 pp., grades 11 and up.

Francis McCullough pulls poems from a wide range of nationalities and many cultures to create a tribute to love for the mature reader. Of the seventy-six poems selected, nearly half are by Asian, African, and Near Eastern poets not frequently represented in English anthologies. Also represented are Russian, Spanish, French, English, and American poets. These are poems of depth and passion that express the various stages of love from the intense joy of "Deep in Love," and "The Song of Solomon," to the excruciating pain of rejection expressed in "Perversity," and "The Fist." Though chosen specifically to appeal to the passion of the young adult, not many are by contemporary authors, and a number of the titles deal with a physical expression of love that may not be appropriate for younger readers. In an effort to avoid a patronizing tone, the anthologist brings together a collection for the thoughtful, sophisticated reader. A table of contents complements indexes to authors, titles, and the first lines of poems.

131 McKuen, Rod, *The Power Bright and Shining: Images of My Country*, Simon and Schuster, 1980 (hardcover), ISBN 0–671–41392–9, 168 pp., grades 10 and up.

Rod McKuen has created a refreshing celebration of what is good and right about America. Even while spelling out many injustices in poems such as "Prejudices," he acknowledges in "Face of Freedom" the value of a land where a determined and inventive people have maintained a passion for freedom. "Out of Darkness" gives an overview of the people who came to settle the land. His queries in "Questions Never Answered" prod the reader to search for answers to keep the nation strong. Although the free-verse poems are long and tend to ramble, sections of them would be a valuable complement to the American history classroom. The language is accessible, though some may object to occasional word choices. Six subject headings organize the collection. These headings are: "Out of the Darkness," "Parading the Colors," "The City," "Citizen's Band," "The Times of Man," and "Set of Instructions." A table of contents gives title access to the selections, and an author's note explains McKuen's philosophy and approach to the subject matter.

132 McNeill, Louise, *Hill Daughter: New and Selected Poems*, ed. Maggie Anderson, University of Pittsburgh Press, 1991 (hardcover), ISBN 0–8229–3685–2, 140 pp., grades 10 and up.

This volume is a labor of love and gratitude compiled by Maggie Anderson. The collection, focusing on the strength of the hill woman, honors author Louise McNeill, who inspired Anderson to write of her own West Virginia background. The variety of styles pays tribute to the talents of the author. Farming, mining, finding oneself, and moving away are a sample of topics covered. A series of poems beginning with "Granny Sanders" traces the lineage of several generations of hill daughters. "Mountain Corn Song" and "Ballad of New River" represent the moods expressed. Although many verses depict the difficult life of mountain dwellers, "Stories at Evening" reveals the nostalgia felt by one who grew up in the secluded environment and thinks back on it with fondness. "Faldang," written with marked cadence, may cause the reader to want to grab a partner and join the dance. Anderson begins the work with a lengthy introduction paying tribute to McNeill's accomplishments. She concludes with author's notes, supplying additional background to eighteen of the selections. A bibliography of McNeill's works and an alphabetical listing of each poem found in the original work conclude the volume.

133 Medearis, Angela Shelf, *Skin Deep and Other Teenage Reflections*, illus. by Michael Bryant, Macmillan Books for Young Readers, 1995 (hardcover), ISBN 0–02–765980–1, 48 pp., grades 6–10.

Medearis has written poems specifically to and about teenagers, whether they come from an urban or a rural setting. Self-concept problems expressed through bulimia are highlighted in "My Mirror Lies to Me." The journey of self-discovery is aptly titled "As Soon as I Know Who I Am You'll Be the First to Know." Serious issues of cultural relations find pen in "Black Barbie Doll," while everyday issues of success or failure at cheerleading tryouts are tackled in "Babies." The simple black and white illustrations by Michael Bryant do not particularly enhance the text. Nor are there any special subject indexes provided. Nonrhyming and succinct, none of the Medearis' verses extend more than one page in length. Rather than guide the reader these poems simply express the emotions of pride, anger, loneliness, and fear common to adolescents. Alternately funny and sad, they ring true to the age group they are intended to reach.

134 Merriam, Eve, *If Only I Could Tell You: Poems for Young Lovers and Dreamers*, Alfred A. Knopf, 1983 (paperback), ISBN 0–394–96043–2, 80 pp., grades 10 and up.

Long known for her contributions to children's verse, Eve Merriam demonstrates her versatility as a writer for young adults in this pocket-sized volume. Written with the empathy of one who must have been composing as a teenager, the author captures the spirit of young love both in bloom and in demise. Variety in length and subject offers enticement for all readers. Writing about a young adult's view of her parent's sometimes-formal responses to each other, Merriam dubs the adults, "Like Bookends" with the child held in the middle. In "Nine Rules I'd Like to Post for My Parents," she gives advice that all mothers and fathers might be wise to follow. "It's Grand" gives a glimpse of how much fun can be had with one of that generation that came *before* parents. The tangible emptiness of missing the beloved is captured in "The Presence of Absence." The thrill of abandonment to love is expressed in "My Acrobatic Circus Dream." The loss of love is reflected in "The Arithmetic Lesson" and "You're Gone." For the young adult who is reluctant to try to find pleasure in reading poetry or thinks that she has nothing to write about, *If Only I Could Tell You* should provide inspiration. Merriam often so powerfully captures the emotion of the moment in as briefly as five lines that it almost takes the breath away.

135 Merriam, Eve, *Rainbow Writing*, Atheneum, 1976 (hardcover), ISBN 0–689–30527–3, 40 pp., grades 9 and up.

Merriam presents here a collection of reflections on life. The mood shifts throughout, even as the flow of life changes, hinging on moments as ephemeral as a rainbow. Selections include "Love Letters, Unmailed" and "Juxtaposing," which mourns the slow death of love. The quiet moments of life, when nature refreshes us and we forget the burdens of the day, are the focus of "The Hill." The light touch of humor will entertain the reader as it crops up in poems like "Aelourophile" and "Aelourophobe." Some selections showcase the delight Merriam takes in playing with words. "Ego-tripping," "Un-negative," and "Misnomer," would be entertaining diversions to bring life to vocabulary lessons. Whoever thought that the simple recitation of the varieties of apples could be as poetic as it is in "Counting-Out Rhyme"? For the teacher trying to reach the student resistant to poetry, Merriam provides the ammunition of a fresh approach.

136 Moon, Pat, *Earth Lines: Poems for the Green Age*, Greenwillow Books, 1991 (hardcover), ISBN 0–688–11853–4, 63 pp., grades 6 and up.

An appreciation for the earth, combined with a concern for its survival, forms the thrust of Pat Moon's verse in *Earth Lines*. Framing his thoughts as questions, in poems like "Danger Sign" and "Litterology," the author forces readers to consider the consequences of personal choices as they relate not only to their personal lives but also to the world around. The irony of "I Am a Tree" and "Eating Disorder," highlight unhealthy societal attitudes toward the earth. Humor proves to be an effective tool in "A Question of Taste" and "Almost Human." Most of the fifty poems are short and straightforward and could appeal to a wide age range. The graphic art illustrations mix photos with pen and ink sketches to support the message of the verse. Moon's introduction explains his purpose in writing this collection. The table of contents aids in accessing the poems.

137 Moore, Lilian, *Poems Have Roots: New Poems*, illus. by Tad Hills, Atheneum Books, 1997 (hardcover), ISBN 0–689–80029–0, 44 pp., grades 6–10.

This pocket-sized book of poems is an expression of the response of the author to the world of nature around her. Having lived on the East Coast as well as the West, the focus of Moore's reflections displays great variety. "Pilgrim Flower" teaches the reader that the pilgrims were responsible for introducing this lacy wildflower to America. "Frogs Are Disappearing" highlights the disappearance of frogs and toads from Yellowstone National Park. "In the Theater of the Sky" rejoices in an aspect of nature that can be enjoyed from anywhere in the country. The tone of the selections alternates between heavy environmental concerns to simple delight at what the poet sees: the full moon, a frozen waterfall, or wind driven clouds. Small black-and-white sketches alternate with gold-toned shadow illustrations throughout the pages. A section titled "Some Notes" at the back of the book explains the background information and experiences that planted the seeds for eleven of the seventeen poems included. As poems have roots in the lives of their creators, so the ideas presented in this volume will grow roots of concern and appreciation in young readers.

138 Mora, Pat, *My Own True Name: New and Selected Poems for Young Adults, 1984–1999*, Arte Publico Press, 2000 (paperback), ISBN 1–55885–292–1, 81 pp., grades 10 and up.

All adolescents struggle with identity issues but for the child born of two cultures, there is yet another dimension to conquer. In this collection Pat Mora speaks from her Mexican-American heart and reveals the struggle to find her "own true name." With the insight of one who has experienced both the richness of a double heritage and the poverty of cultural rejection, the author brings her readers face to face, skin to skin with living biracially. In "Mango Juice" and "Ode to Pizza" food is not merely eaten, but is celebrated. "1910" demonstrates the explosive result of prejudice, while "Sugar" previews the simmering poison of the same. "Two Worlds" reflects the rejection endured by those whose skin is neither quite white nor dark brown, while "Desert Women" rejoices in the resilient beauty of ladies whose flesh is naturally tanned and enhanced by the sun.

From the opening pages, Mora reaches out to connect with her audience. Her unique introduction addresses her readers with, "Dear Fellow Writer." This letter offers encouraging admonitions to aspiring authors. In the body of the work, the poems are grouped under metaphorical titles—"Blooms," "Thorns," and "Roots"—representing living, growing things. This anthology was fifteen years in the making and contains some new verses as well as selections from Mora's previous works—*Chants*, *Borders*, and *Communion*. Every library should have a copy of this little volume. It is rich with life lessons in survival, acceptance, courage, and determination, all expressed in the language of tenderness and beauty.

139 Morgan, Robert, *At the Edge of the Orchard Country*, Wesleyan University Press, 1987 (paperback), ISBN 0–8195–6164–9, 68 pp., grades 10 and up.

With earthy reverence and respect, Robert Morgan writes of his mountain heritage. In more than forty free verse offerings, he paints seasons, rituals, relationships, recreation, and the strength to survive in the Blue Ridge Mountains. "White Autumn" describes the indomitable woman of the hills who defeated every crisis she faced and whose only weakness was a love of reading. "Potato Hole" pictures the security of a hideaway vegetable cellar where a boy could escape from the world. "Nail Bag" provides a glimpse of pioneer families with values decidedly different from those of contemporary society. Poems are grouped into three chapters with the final section focusing entirely on the history of the area. Morgan gives an intimate and inviting view of rural mountain life. For young adults who live in this geographical area, his works may open new doors to an appreciation of literature as it relates to their reality. For urban readers, these verses will be culturally enlightening.

140 Morgan, Robert, *Red Owl*, W. W. Norton and Company, 1972 (paperback), ISBN 0–393–04136–0, 73 pp., grades 8 and up.

Unpretentious in style and presentation, *Red Owl* is nevertheless a lovely book. In selections such as "House Burning" and "Well," Robert Morgan's poetry says as much by implication as by declaration. While writing about the everyday subjects of topsoil, muddy roads, and the thawing of the ground, he reminds the reader continually of the power of nature that influences the lives of man. An overriding sense of respect and appreciation for the earth and a need for solitary time to enjoy its beauty fill these pages. Short and conversational in style, these poems convey the essence of life in the southern Appalachians. Titles listed in the table of contents are divided into three sections but seem to have no specific subject correlation. An acknowledgments page lists other sources that have printed the author's poems.

141 Morrison, Lillian, ed., *At the Crack of the Bat*, illus. by Steve Cieslawski, Hyperion Books for Children, 1992 (hardcover), ISBN 1–56282–176–8, 63 pp., grades 8–12.

If there lingers a question of which sport is the national pastime, Morrison's collection of forty-four poems will knock it out of the park. From the opening plea of "Take Me Out to the Ball Game," to the wistful end of season, "October," the thrill of the game is expressed. It would seem that Morrison has thoroughly researched the annals of both the sport and verse to pull together this anthology. Hall of Fame winners from the 1930s and 1940s are immortalized in "Baseball's Sad Lexicon" and "Tinker to Evers." Heroes of the field are honored in "Hammerin' Hank," "For Junior Gilliam (1928–1978)," "The Great One," "Mister October, Reggie Jackson," "Nolan Ryan," and a number of other poems. Specific teams, "The Red Stockings"; unforgettable plays, "Winner"; trading cards, "The Baseball Card Dealer"; and many other aspects of this popular sport are included.

Special features adding a broader dimension to the reader's enjoyment are Cieslawski's profuse portrait quality illustrations in vibrant colors as well as sepia line drawings. A "Notes on Ballplayers" section supplies information about specific players from Babe Ruth to Nolan Ryan.

142 Morrison, Lillian, comp., *Best Wishes, Amen: A New Collection of Autograph Verses*, illus. by Loretta Lustig, Thomas Y. Crowell, 1974 (hardcover), ISBN 0–690–00579–2, 195 pp., grades 7 and up.

For more than fifty years Lillian Morrison has been collecting the potpourri of thoughts such as those found in this collection. Two previous volumes were published in 1950 and 1961. In her introduction, she traces the history of autograph verses, noting that many date back to ancient civilizations and yet are as current as a contemporary pun. Subclassifications of the genre are as varied as compliments, insults, moral advice, sentimental wishes, and puns. Topics cover the basics of life: personality, success, school, love, and marriage. These brief verses reflect the youthful mind in its unposed, unpretentious reality.

In this collection entries are most often untitled, as autographs would be. Morrison gives some structure by dividing the little quips into twelve chapters. The chapter entitled "May Your Life Be Like Spaghetti" contains the title verse, "Excuse the Writing, Blame the Pen. Best Wishes, Amen." Morrison introduces the anthology with the history of autograph verse. The work concludes with an acknowledgments section referencing the authors of the 325 selections. There are also brief biographical sketches of Morrison and Lustig.

143 Morrison, Lillian, *The Break Dance Kids: Poems of Sport, Motion and Locomotion*, Lothrop, Lee and Shepard Books, 1985 (hardcover), ISBN 0–688–045545, 63 pp., grades 8 and up.

Although the photographs that illustrate this small volume are dated by 1970s and 1980s hairstyles and clothes, the twenty-first century young adult will relate to many of the verses, since the themes of sport and motion are timeless and always popular with many members of the young adult audience. The thirty-five poems are not divided into chapters but rather are listed individually in the table of contents. There is an almost one-to-one ratio of illustration to text as photographs give visual substance to most of the poems. The topics of dance, sports heroes, children, and nature are all represented. However, the emphasis on sports predominates, with activities ranging from tennis to boxing. This little volume has a double appeal for the young adult. Focusing on the facets of life that require the most motion—sports and dance—is a natural hook for the active young person, and the easily memorized brief verses should find a home in the teen reader's heart. The only special feature is a listing of other works, current to 1985, by Lillian Morrison. However, after discovering these verses, the young adult reader may find that information to be very valuable.

144 Morrison, Lillian, ed,. *Rhythm Road: Poems to Move To*, Lothrop, Lee and Shepard Books, 1988 (hardcover), ISBN 0–688–07098–1, 148 pp., grades 9 and up.

Morrison's choice of a title for this collection reveals the criterion for each verse included. From dance to technology, from nature to war, movement and motion are felt. Sixty-eight poets are represented in the ten chapters. Intriguing chapter titles such as "Oompah on the Tuba" and "The Rusty Spigot Sputters" inspire even the most active young adult to pause and read on. Contributors range from Thomas Hood, with a selection from "The Song of the Shirt" and its focus on work, to Shel Silverstein's celebration of a favorite holiday in "The

Fourth." Special helps include an index of titles, an index of first lines, and an index of authors. Copyright credits list sources for each selection.

145 Morrison, Lillian, *The Sidewalk Racer, and Other Poems of Sports and Motion*, Lothrop, Lee and Shepard Co, 1977 (hardcover), ISBN 0–688–41805–8, 62 pp. grades 9 and up.

For the sports enthusiast, Morrison's anthology will be enticing. The sheer exhilaration of motion and exertion to excellence shine in poems like "The Angel's of Motion." Here the editor has collected verse not only to extol the fluid beauty of sport, but also to expose the emotional impact of these activities. There is hardly a sport omitted. Whether it be a team sport such as football in "Passing Fair," or an individual effort, as in "On Our Bikes," a great many physical activities are represented here. Morrison defends her love of sports by comparing the rhythm of poetry to that found in sports. As she reminds the reader, sports and poetry both elicit strong emotions from the participant. The poems in this small volume are easily understood and should find a niche in the high school classroom.

146 Morrison, Lillian, comp., *Sprints and Distances*, illus. by Clare and John Ross, Thomas Y. Crowell Company, 1965 (hardcover), ISBN 0–690–76571–1, 211 pp., grades 8 and up.

Lillian Morrison's introduction to this anthology, though written in prose, is almost poetry in narrative form. She draws parallels in design and execution to sport and verse—the discipline, emotion, drive, and power. Shared with students, this brief piece is in itself a magnet to pull even the reluctant into reading. Her prefatory note gives an overview of sources from Virgil to Ogden Nash. Morrison also previews the mood of the selections from dedication to satire in these explanatory pages. Nearly 150 contributors cover a variety of sports. Those enjoyed by teams and spectators alike such as baseball, football, rugby, and swimming are represented by numerous titles. Those skills that have survived the test of time, such as falconry, fencing, boating, and hunting, are also noted. For the solitary sportsman or woman, there are verses reflecting on fishing, kite flying, walking, and climbing. On land, water, and in the air, through talent, strength, and endurance, tribute is paid to a total of twenty-five categories of sports. Eight chapter divisions are listed by topic, not by sport, and celebrate the unity of feeling in victory, loss, or the preparation for an event. Special features concluding the volume are an acknowledgments page, an index of authors, index of first lines, index of titles, and an index by sport.

147 Myers, Walter Dean, *Harlem: A Poem*, illus. by Christopher Myers, Scholastic Press, 1977 (hardcover), ISBN 0–590–54340–7, unpaged, grades 9 and up.

Walter Dean Myers' single volume poem is a celebration of the flesh and the soul of Harlem. Expressing both the divergence and the unity of experience this unique community demonstrates, Myers has created a living, breathing tapestry of color and sound. The food, the street games, the worship, the struggle, and the music woven throughout paint a vibrant picture of this important portion of American culture. Winning a Caldecott Honor award in 1988, Christopher Myers' brightly hued collages provide a powerful accent to the lyrical verse. Although published in picture book format, this is not a book just for children. The older the reader, the more understanding they will have of the images presented.

148 Nash, Ogden, comp., *The Moon Is Shining Bright as Day*, illus. by Rose Shirvanian, J.B. Lippincott Company, 1953 (hardcover), ISBN 0–397–30244–4, 176 pp., grades 6 and up.

It is difficult to conceive of a poetry collection that omits Ogden Nash. In this volume, Nash is both contributor and compiler. The beloved humorist has brought together those verses that represent his favorites for young people. The works of nearly one hundred writers from both sides of the Atlantic are represented. Authors range from A.A. Milne to Henry Wadsworth Longfellow. Nash acknowledges that the chief criterion for his selections was that he liked them.

Six chapters, titled by lines from poems, form the framework for the anthology. Most of the works are classics. Arthur Guiterman gives a terse lesson in etiquette in "Of Tact." The thrill and wanderlust created by the sound of a distant train is reflected in Edna St. Vincent Millay's "Travel." Ogden Nash's familiar admonition for safety is expressed in "The Panther." Some word choices may seem archaic to the twenty-first century young reader, but there is enough beauty in the lines or humor or wisdom in each piece to make the anthology a treasured find. The collection concludes with indexes of authors, titles, and first lines. Acknowledgment of sources for the material are located at the beginning of the volume.

149 Nye, Naomi Shihab, and Paul B. Janeczko, eds. *I Feel a Little Jumpy Around You*, Simon and Schuster Books for Young Readers, 1996 (hardcover), ISBN 0–689–80518–7, 256 pp., grades 9 and up.

This expansive collection of more than two hundred poems has the unique potential to bridge the gender gap, or at least clarify some issues that have traditionally remained cloudy. Nye and Janeczko bring to this work their own credentials as writers for young adults.

This anthology includes more than 150 writers from all over the world. Some are well known while others are just arriving on the publishing scene. Male and female poets are paired and juxtaposed with ideas, insights, views, and voices both harmonious and discordant. A sampling of contributors—Rita Dove, Edward Hirsch, Jacinto Jesus Cardona, George Ella Lyon, Grace Paley—indicates the variety in perspective. There is something here to match each mood, running the gamut from delight to mourning; from anger to joy.

Four main sections with the provocative titles of "Heads on Fire," "Foreign Exchange," "The Real Names of Everything," and "Separate Longings," provide the framework for poems covering topics ranging from the first kiss to relationships with grandparents. If there were one word that would describe this anthology it would be "relationships." Whether the connection is with a parent, a sweetheart (lost or found), sibling, mate, or even with one's self, the innate ingredient is relationship.

Unique features provide significant support for the text. First are creatively composed dual introductions. Just reading the cryptic comments is enough to whet the appetite for other collections by each editor. The main body of work follows. "Contributor's Notes" offer a personalized attraction and contain direct quotes from each of the poets in response to a list of questions sent by the editors. These vignettes give insight to the reason behind the writing. Again, Nye and Janeczko have a sort of "last word" dialogue with each other as a footnote to each of these pages. To conclude, there is an acknowledgment page citing the works quoted in the text. An index of poems, index to female poets, and index to male poets complete the supplementary material.

150 Nye, Naomi Shihab, comp., *Salting the Ocean: 100 Poems by Young Poets*, illus. by Ashley Bryan, Greenwillow Books, 2000 (hardcover), ISBN 0–688–16193–6, 111 pp., grades 6 and up.

Drawing from her twenty-five years of teaching poetry in schools, Nye has put together a collection of verse written by students in grades one to twelve. Poems are divided into four groups. "My Shadow Is an Ant" contains poems about the inner world where feelings of rejection and inadequacy are found in titles like "Remember" and "I Feel Like a Puppy." Titles in "Think How Many Stones Are in Your Shirt" focus on where students live. "My Grandma Squashes Roaches with Her Hand" features verses that highlight family relationships. "Pictures" speaks of the security of parental love. "In the Morning" shows the insecurity and fears caused by an atmosphere of anger. The final section, which gives space to the "wide imagination," tells of the need for solitude in "Where

Does My Free Time Go?" and ponders the stages of life in "Growing is Like. . . ." It is titled "Silence Is Like a Tractor Moving the Whole World."

Numerous features aid the reader in accessing not only the contents, but the essence of this volume. A lengthy introduction explains how the collection came to be published, encourages parents and teachers to expose their children to poetry, and instructs future poets how to give space to their creative urges. For those interested in pursuing poetry further, there is a list of suggestions for further reading. Indexes list both poems and poets. Colorful stylistic illustrations featuring multicultural images introduce each section of poems. The quality of the verse is uneven, but many are worthy of attention. They certainly should help attain Nye's goal of encouraging students to gain a sense of their own voice.

151 Nye, Naomi Shihab, comp., *The Space Between Our Footsteps: Poems and Paintings from the Middle East*, Simon and Schuster Books For Young Readers, 1998 (hardcover), ISBN 0–689–81233–7, 144 pp., grades 8 and up.

In her expansive anthology Naomi Shihab Nye has gathered the work of numerous writers and illustrators from the Middle East for a virtual feast of verse. The menu lists contributors from Yemen, United Arab Emirates, Turkey, Tunisia, Syria, Saudi Arabia, Qatar, Kuwait, Jordan, Israel, Iraq, Iran, Egypt, Bahrain, and Algeria. Each work is translated from the native tongue. A colorful and easily read map shows the location of each country. Brief biographical sketches provide a more intimate picture of individual authors. Nye shares a tempting taste of these cultures with her English-speaking audience. Topics include an appreciation for childhood and tenderness toward children; devotion to family and homeland; the pain of exile; respect for nature, and one's fellow man; and a general love of life. These themes reflect images from Nye's childhood when her Palestinian father kept his culture alive through nightly storytelling.

Poems include those that feature the topics of faith, "Two Hands on the Water"; family, "I Remember My Father's Hands"; extended family, "My Uncle Wore a Rose on His Lapel"; heritage, "Bethlehem"; literature, "The Bridge"; and many others. Each contribution portrays a fresh view of a culture that remains enigmatic to many American readers. Nye characterizes her collection as an artistic response to the frequent negativism and sensationalism expressed in the media. She desires to exchange "news" that goes deeper than the headlines. This collection is so personal and authentic that the reader can almost smell the rich coffee being poured, hear the sizzling of pine nuts in olive oil, and experience the hospitality of the Eastern household.

152 Nye, Naomi Shihab, comp., *This Same Sky: A Collection of Poems from Around the World*, Four Winds Press, 1992 (hardcover), ISBN 0–02–768440–7, 212 pp., grades 8 and up.

As the sky stretches over all, so there are emotions and responses common to people, yet new voices share fresh truths. This is the premise upon which this collection is based—universal feelings finding unique expression. Nye has included 129 contributors—some are well known internationally, others are novices with initial submissions. Some selections were originally written in English, others are in translation. It is Nye's purpose in this volume to show readers what lies beyond familiar borders and, for that reason, she has deliberately omitted writers from the United States. The work is divided into six chapters with titles that reinforce the universality of some experiences. The chapter "Words and Silences," in which "The Meaning of Simplicity," a translated piece by Yannis Ritsos appears, states the philosophy of the entire anthology. "Dreams and Dreamers" includes "On My Birthday," a selection from Bangladesh by Farhad Mazhar extolling the virtues of one's own special day. The chapter entitled "Families" covers thirty pages of individual experiences—both positive and negative. In "This Earth and Sky in Which We Live" nearly every aspect of nature is examined in close to fifty pages of verse. The chapter entitled "Losses" addresses a variety of topics from nature through human growth. Finally, "Human Mysteries" contains verses ranging from self-discovery in "Goodness" by Benny Andersen, a translated verse from Denmark, to "Or" by Ali Darwish, with its observations of life, which is a translated verse from Egypt.

Special features introduce and close the work. Naomi Shihab Nye provides an inviting introduction enlarging on the purpose of the work. Brief anecdotes on each of the contributors, a world map noting locations of contributors, suggestions for further reading, acknowledgments, an index to countries, and an index to poets round out the text.

153 Nye, Naomi Shihab, *The Tree Is Older Than You Are: A Bilingual Gathering of Poems and Stories from Mexico with Paintings by Mexican Artists*, Simon and Schuster Books for Young Readers, 1995 (hardcover), ISBN 0–689–80297–8, 112 pp., grades 10 and up.

This volume of 102 poems and folktales of Mexican writers, which is accented by illustrations of sixty-four Mexican artists, includes numerous aids. An index of titles in English is followed by an index to titles in Spanish and an index of writers and artists. Background notes cover each literary and artistic contributor. There is a note on each folktale included and a note on the translations and translators. Finally, there is a list of illustrations.

The collection is divided into two sections entitled "People: 'Rub the Leaves in Your Hands'," and "Earth and Animals 'Impulse of Roots'." Topics covered deal with universal themes of nature as in "I Am a Peach Tree," "The Turtle," "Brother Sun," and "The Woodpecker." Others touch on family issues in "Mothers with a Baby" and "In the Silver." Works included are by such renowned authors as Octavio Paz, Alberto Blanco, and Rosario Castellanos as well as newer poets, some of whom are still in their youth. English translations are presented side-by-side with the original Mexican poems and legends. The illustrations, which are reproductions of paintings by various artists, are not meant to be literal interpretations of the poems but represent a spectrum of Mexican artists. Some works the compiler has chosen are obscure and others straightforward, but all combine to give the reader a strong flavor of Mexican literature and art.

154 Nye, Naomi Shihab, ed., *what have you lost?* photo. by Michael Nye, Greenwillow Books, 1999 (hardcover), ISBN 0–688–16184–7, 205 pp., grades 10 and up.

Realizing early in life that experiencing loss is inevitable, Nye has collected poems over many years that speak to this most basic human condition. Losses covered in the resulting anthology of 140 poets range from those that are petty to those that are disastrous. The discomfort experienced after losing personal items sold in a garage sale stand next to the emotions of loss experienced in making the necessary adjustments to a new culture and the feelings of grief thrust upon someone after the suicide of a young boy. Some selections are depressing, some hopeful, some wistful, some regretful, some resigned, and some angry, but through them all the subject of loss is thoroughly explored. Poets are a mix of new and well-known, but the format is basically free verse. Many require thoughtful consideration and would benefit from class discussion.

Illustrative portraits by Michael Nye are not literal interpretations of the poems, but are photo essays telling stories in and of themselves. The editor's notes at the beginning of the book provide a helpful introduction to the subject of loss and give the reader a sense of direction in reading the poems included. An index to poets, an index to poems, as well as a subject index to the particular losses addressed by the selections are also helpful. Of special interest are the fifteen pages of notes on the lives of the contributors, which are arranged in alphabetical order by the poet's names.

155 Okutoro, Lydia Omolola, comp., *Quiet Storm: Voices of Young Black Poets*, Hyperion Books for Children, 1999 (hardcover), ISBN 0–7868–0461–0, 102 pp., grades 9 and up.

Okutoro groups the poems she has selected for inclusion in *Quiet Storm* by theme. Each section of poetry, which represents young adults from a variety of

African heritages, is introduced with a work by well-known poets such as Langston Hughes and Nikki Giovanni. Chapter headings include "Wearing Our Pride," "We the Observers," "Motherlands and the 'Hood," "Trip to My Soul," "Love Rhythms," "The Struggle Continues," "After Tomorrow," and "To Our Elders." With the ages of the poets ranging from thirteen to twenty-one, the quality of the writing remains consistently high. The observations made are insightful and challenging. With the broad range of issues addressed, young people of all cultures will find a point of connection. Despite the serious content of many of the verses, the overall mood of the collection remains upbeat and positive. The compiler begins with an introduction and closes with an extensive section "About the Poets," which gives background information about each of the fifty poets included in the anthology. Reading of other young poets may encourage the faint-at-heart to try their own hand at expressing their thoughts through verse.

156 Panzer, Nora, ed., *Celebrate America in Poetry and Art*, Hyperion Paperbacks for Children, 1999 (paperback), ISBN 0–7868–1360–1, 96 pp., grades 7 and up.

This collection might be called a medley of America's greatest hits in verse and on canvas. Celebrating diversity, this anthology also brings together the words and brush stokes of the country's most accomplished writers and artists to provide a cross-country tour of America's landscapes, both physical and ethnic. The five divisions of the book highlight natural beauty, the many branched heritage of America's family tree, construction of towns and villages, protest and struggle, and the simple heartbeat of everyday life. Illustrations all are taken from the National Museum of American Art, Smithsonian Institution.

A sampling from the forty-nine writers and fifty-one artists includes Maurice Kenny writing of the Native American heritage in "Legacy," depicted in art by George Catlin in "River Bluffs, 1320 Miles above St. Louis." Carl Sandburg gives a poet's eye view of one of nature's wonders in "Niagara," with an accompanying painting of the same name by George Inness. Leslie Nelson Jennings portrays a time when just sitting and thinking was greatly valued in "Front Porch," illustrated by Frank Blackwell Mayer's "Independence (Squire Jack Porter)." Confrontation has also been a part of America, and Joseph Seaman Cotter Jr.'s "Sonnet to Negro Soldiers" is representative of battle with its illustration "Under Fire" by William Johnson.

The work concludes with biographical notes, giving information on each of the writers and artists. There is also a reference section listing illustrations with a brief explanation of the source, dimensions in the actual museum display, and the medium used in the piece. The source of each of the verses is listed in an acknowledgments division. Finally, there is an index including titles of works and their creators.

157 Paulos, Martha, comp. and illus., *Felines: Great Poets on Notorious Cats*, Chronicle Books, 1992 (hardcover), ISBN 0–8118–0103–9, 63 pp., grades 8 and up.

For the reader who holds affection for cats, this collection of twenty poems will bring delight in a variety of forms. Well-known writers crossing time, gender, and ethnic lines are contributors. Martha Paulos adorns alternating pages with her active and amusing linocuts. Intriguing facets of the ever enigmatic feline are explored. William Wordsworth pictures the playful side in 'Kitten and the Fallen Leaves." Don Marquis explores the possibility that even in sleep one's pet is dreaming of more violent ancestors in "The Tom Cat." John Ciardi expresses the exasperation of all cat owners when a pet can't decide whether to be in or out in "My Cat Mrs. Lick-a-chin." Paul Gallico humorously tackles the often-faced question of ownership in "This Is My Chair." The partnership of illustrator and accomplished writers makes this little anthology a pleasant addition to collections of animal verse.

158 Paulos, Martha, ed. and illus., *insectAsides*, Viking Studio Books, 1994 (hardcover), ISBN 0–670–85567–7, 54 pp., grades 7 and up.

The young adult with a scientific bent who may find most poetry pointless or tedious may develop a new appreciation for verse after reading this unique collection. Paulos, remaining true to her previous collections, *Doggerel* and *Felines*, begins by creating a pun with the title. She then shares eighteen poems by traditional and contemporary writers, accompanied by her bright linocut illustrations. Don Marquis writes of an ill-fated entertainer in "the flattered lightning bug." Ogden Nash expresses more empathetic thoughts in "the ant." Robert Frost salutes the intellect of a fly in "a considerable speck." This little entomological find provides a delightful connection between biology and literature and should prove a valuable classroom resource for the teacher interested in coordinating the two subjects. End pages are decorated with dozens of bustling ants. Acknowledgments are given on the copyright page.

159 Peck, Richard, ed., *Mindscapes: Poems for the Real World*, Delacorte Press, 1971 (hardcover), ISBN 0–440–05644–6, 165 pp., grades 9 and up.

In *Mindscapes*, Richard Peck has created an anthology of poems that are accessible rather than mysterious. Cutting a wide swathe across time periods from W.B. Yeats to Robert Frost to Rod McKuen, the compiler has chosen selections that speak to the present. Topics as everyday as "The High School Band" find space next to those that examine eternal issues as in "The Vanity of Human Wishes" and "To An Athlete Dying Young." Young adults especially will relate to the need for independence and solitude expressed in "Freedom." Many of the poets included reject the structures of rhyme and iambic pentameter in favor of lines that provide more immediate communication. An index of authors and an index of first lines make the selections easy to find. With these eleven chapters, every young person should be able to find something to please.

160   Peck, Richard, ed. *Sounds and Silences*, Delacorte Press, 1970 (paperback), ISBN 0–440–98171–9, 177 pp., grades 10 and up.

Reflecting the era in which it was compiled, this collection of verses expresses the realities of life as seen in the 1960s and 1970s. However, the themes are timeless. Editor Richard Peck elaborates on the criteria for his selections in an informal introduction. A look at the table of contents reveals the general thrust of the anthology. The twelve chapter titles depict the range of themes—from "The Family" and "Childhood" on through "Illusion," "Dissent," and "War." Contributions by more than fifty poets, predominately from the contemporary period, also demonstrate variety—from William Butler Yeats to the Beatles. Advice from parents such as "Mother to Son" by Langston Hughes and "What Shall He Tell That Son?" by Carl Sandburg are samples from the chapter entitled "The Family." Lyrics from the familiar folksong "Where Have All the Flowers Gone" by Pete Seeger reflect feelings of protesters in the chapter focusing on war. George Barker pays touching tribute in "Sonnet To My Mother" in the final chapter, "Recollections." The volume concludes with an index of first lines, an index of authors and titles, and an acknowledgments page.

161   Philip, Neil, ed., *Singing America: Poems That Define a Nation*, illus. by Michael McCurdy, Viking, 1995 (hardcover), ISBN 0–670–86150–2, 160 pp., grades 8 and up.

Along with accepted American poets such as Walt Whitman and Langston Hughes, offerings in Philip's anthology include works by lyricist Woody Guthrie and Native American voices. Traditional spirituals and songs of the Pueblo and Sioux are interspersed with anthems and verse. Through these selections the editor presents the reader with a broad-reaching historical panorama useful to the teacher who is attempting to incorporate literature with the study of this country's past. Poems, though not in strict chronological order, are generally arranged from early history to recent history. They showcase the development of American poetry beginning with Whitman and include poets speaking in the vernacular of America.

The picture of America, that is presented is multicultural, but the language of some selections may be looked on as less than sensitive by today's standards. Woodcut illustrations by Michael McCurdy add sophistication and energy to the volume. Three indexes are included for the reader's guidance: an index to poets, an index of titles and first lines, and a subject index. Another helpful feature is the list of additional volumes of American poetry. This volume could be a valuable tool to encourage young people to consider not only what America has been but how they will create it to be in the future.

162   Philip, Neil, ed., *War and the Pity of War*, illus. by Michael McCurdy, Clarion Books, 1998 (hardcover), ISBN 0–395–84982–9, 96 pp., grades 10 and up.

Philip begins his anthology with an introduction that examines the changing attitudes toward war since 1914. He delineates the switch from viewing armed conflict as a noble endeavor to seeing it as a tragic waste of men's lives. The titles he has chosen further emphasize the horror rather than the heroism of war.
Selections begin in 800–600 B.C. with the Chinese offering, "How Few of Us Are Left, How Few!" and continue through the recent Serbo-Croatian conflict in "Essential Serbo-Croat." "The Charge of the Light Brigade" and "John Brown's Body" are among the well-known choices included, but many of the titles are less familiar. World Wars I and II are heavily represented as is the Vietnam War. Obviously missing are the American and French Revolutions. Michael McCurdy's strikingly somber scratchboard illustrations drive home the devastatingly high price of war. This volume would be appropriate to use as a tie-in to secondary history classes. Indexes to titles and first lines are provided.

163   Plotz, Helen, comp., *Imagination's Other Place: Poems of Science and Mathematics*, illus. by Clare Leighton, Thomas Y. Crowell, 1955 (hardcover), ISBN 0–690–04700–2, 200 pp., grades 9 and up.

Based on the premise that science and art are virtually two sides of the same coin, and that coin is imagination, Helen Plotz brings together verses rooted in the same foundation. Branching out from a common source, the explorer and the creator both want to communicate, both thrive on order, and both have vision. Innately, both seek insight and must have foresight to succeed. This collection of verses, then, focuses on the topics of science and mathematics as well as contributors to those fields of thought. Specific disciplines included are astronomy, geography, physics, mathematics, chemistry, biology, and medicine. No doubt, some discoveries may be outdated in the twenty-first century, but other facts remain untouched by time.
Claude Bragdon observes provocative parallels in geometry and botany in "The Point, the Line, the Surface and Sphere." David McCord discovers music in the names of winds in "Weather Words." Emma Rounds has fun with "Plane Geometry," her parody of Lewis Carrolls' "Jabberwocky." More than seventy authors from both sides of the Atlantic contribute to the nearly one hundred

selections. Special features include a preface stating the purpose of the anthology, acknowledgments pages, and indexes of authors, titles, and first lines. Young adults with an interest in the sciences as well as teachers of those subjects will find this unique collection to be inviting.

164 Pollinger, Gina, sel., *Something Rich and Strange: A Treasury of Shakespeare's Verse*, illus. by Emma Chichester Clark, Kingfisher, 1995 (hardcover), ISBN 1–85697–597–5, 95 pp., grades 7 and up.

Gina Pollinger rises to the formidable yet rewarding task of gleaning the choicest fruit from the bountiful harvest of Shakespeare. The more than two hundred short poems will whet the appetite of young adults for heartier fare. Pollinger reminds readers that even though the lines are written in sixteenth-century vernacular, the subjects are familiar, even commonplace to the contemporary audience. Human behavior depicted in love, war, humor, betrayal, and other passions is timeless and remains unchanged across the ages. It is Pollinger's desire to make Shakespeare accessible to the modern reader.

Selections are grouped by theme. Each play or poem from which lines have been lifted is credited. The fact that the beauty and flow of the verses shines through even without the surrounding text demonstrates the genius of the Bard of Avon. End pages bear line upon line of familiar quotes, each standing alone yet speaking with power. Emma Clark's vignettes decorate each page of the text. Special helps include a table of contents; a biographical sketch of Shakespeare; indexes of plays, poetry, and first lines; and a glossary. This is a work that is meant to be savored for its richness and to be read aloud to achieve its full effect.

165 Ray, David and Judy Ray, eds. *Fathers: A Collection of Poems*, St. Martin's Griffin, 1997 (paperback), ISBN 0–312–20964–9, 254 pp., grades 10 and up.

In this anthology the Rays have assembled thoughts on fathers and fatherhood culled from 118 renowned American poets. They focus on fathers both present and absent, those who helped, as well as those who hurt, even sharing a bit of their own backgrounds. A detailed introduction explains the significance of this collection. The editors remind readers of the psychological implications of having both child and father housed in the same body—which they say is true of everyone. Although this collection was prepared for an older audience, young adults will find selections from this anthology that connect with their own experiences. A natural result of reading these poems may be writing of one's own father, stepfather, or grandfather. The Rays also encourage readers to respond to them and express their feelings about their own fathers as well as their reaction to this book.

Contributors to this work include William Stafford ("A Story That Could Be True"), Gwendolyn Brooks ("In Honor of David Anderson Brooks, My Father"), Judith Vollmer ("Father's Magic Trick"), Dan Brown ("As Seen at the Uffizi"), Robert Bly ("My Father at Eighty-Five"), and many others. Special features include a section entitled "Notes on the Poets (And Their Fathers)," which is self-explanatory.

166 Rogansky, Barbara, ed., *Winter Poems*, illus. by Trina Schart Hyman, Scholastic Inc., 1994 (hardcover), ISBN 0–590–42873–X, 40 pp., grades 7 and up.

Barbara Rogansky introduces this memorable collection of seasonal verses by expressing her love for both winter and poetry, thus setting the stage for a work of the heart. Even if each of the twenty-five selections is already known to the reader, it is worth owning this book for the right to return at will to the beautifully crisp illustrations. Trina Schart Hyman, award-winning artist, captures each verse with her signature style. The unique feature of these miniature masterpieces is that the house and the surrounding countryside are home to compiler and illustrator. Hyman, Rogansky, and other family members are subjects of the art work.

Selections range from the contemporary lines written by David Kheridan for his wife, Nonny, to the ancient five-line Japanese verse from 905 A.D. Offerings that may surprise readers are "A Merry Note" by William Shakespeare and a cheerful excerpt from "The Bells" by Edgar Allan Poe. Other more familiar works include "Something Told the Wild Geese" by Rachel Field and "Cat on a Night of Snow" by Elizabeth Coatsworth. For those who consider the winds and bare limbs of winter to be depressing and dreary, this depiction of the season will surely bring a new view.

167 Rosenberg, Liz, ed., *Earth-Shattering Poems*, Henry Holt and Company, 1998 (hardcover), ISBN 0–8050–4821–9, 126 pp., grades 9 and up.

There are experiences in life that prose cannot begin to describe. The intensity of emotion is so great that only poetry can adequately give release to the soul. Poems of such earth-shattering moments are collected in this small volume compiled by Liz Rosenberg. Poems of love, loss, pain, and joy are gathered from all over the world and from all time periods. Beginning with Sappho, born in the Greek isles in 620 B.C., Rosenberg adds poets such as William Blake from the 1700s, William Butler Yeats of the 1800s, and Langston Hughes and Sylvia Plath of the 1900s. Their places of origin extend from Ancient China to Russia during Stalin's reign of terror, Spain at the time of the Civil War, Peru, El Salvador, Germany, France, Great Britain, Japan, and America. Gathered in one volume especially for young people, these poems are a good match for the stormy days of young adulthood when extreme joy, sorrow, and confusion all follow hard one upon another. Rosenberg believes that poetry cannot be forced, but must be found when the time is right and that youth is often the appropriate time.

Extensive biographical notes about each poet's life and contribution to the field give insight to the meaning of the poems included. An additional section lists books of and about poetry that may be of interest to the reader. The work concludes with an index of authors and an index of first lines. The editor states that she has included only a sample of the poems she loves best. Some are dark, some joyous, some filled with laughter and others with pain, but all speak to those "earth-shattering" moments that invade all of our lives.

168 Rosenberg, Liz, ed., *The Invisible Ladder*, Henry Holt and Company, 1996 (hardcover), ISBN 0–8050–3836–1, 210 pp., grades 10 and up.

Liz Rosenberg has demonstrated in this anthology what writers avow over and over again: that writing poetry is an expression of the child still residing in the adult. She also proves that for many works, there is no age boundary. In this collection she offers poems generally considered to be written for adults, but that in reality are enjoyed by all ages. Her format includes black and white photographs of each contributor as a child and as an adult with commentary on childhood events that influenced each author's choice in becoming a writer. For the teacher who is in search of what connects poetry to life, the authors' observations are a gold mine.

The thirty-nine writers represent a broad base of contemporary verse. Marvin Bell pays tribute to a ladylove with "To Dorothy." David Chin shares a family portrait with "Sleeping Father." Martin Espada makes a cryptic observation in "Courthouse Graffiti for Two Voices." Linda Pastan gives a new outlook on an old food in "Egg." Jane O. Wayne adds a new dimension to chores and homework in "In Praise of Zigzags." Robley Wilson's "I Wish in the City of Your Heart" was the inspiration for the entire work, while Diana Rivera's "Dinner Together" carries the title for the collection.

Rosenberg concludes with a five-page section on "Ways to Use This Book." She encourages students and teachers to write to her and share thoughts based on Wilson's poem. Her enthusiasm for reading and writing poetry will spark new ideas in the curriculum weary teacher. Other useful features include biographical notes on each author and an index of first lines.

169 Rosenberg, Liz, ed., *Light-Gathering Poems*, Henry Holt and Company, 2000 (hardcover), ISBN 0–8050–6223–8, 146 pp., grades 8 and up.

Acting as the light gatherer, Liz Rosenberg harvests verses that radiate encouragement. In her introduction she advises readers that this is a companion volume to *Earth-Shattering Poems*, which takes as its theme broken dreams, death, and other painful experiences. This volume then brings wholeness, healing, and beauty.

Selections come from all over the globe and include translations from Raner Marie Rilke, Armado Nervo, Issa, and others. Also timeless, the verses are gleaned from the Psalms of the Bible and recent writers of the twentieth and twenty-first centuries. The connecting thread is always light—whether actual or metaphorical. Rabindranath Tagore writes of tiny sparkles in lines from "Fireflies." Ruth Stone illumines precious family moments with "Green Apples." Christina Rossetti encourages gentle brightness in "Hurt No Living Thing." William Butler Yeats even adds a light touch to the Pearly Gates with "The Fiddler of Dooney." With the dark specters of homelessness, abuse, and ecological disaster rampant at the dawning of a new century, Rosenberg's collection brings with it a prism of hope and brightness.

Special features are almost as much a treasure as is the text. Biographical notes with their informative annotations of authors' lives cover more than thirty pages. Concluding each vignette is a list of suggested readings by or about the author. This is a work that both middle and high school teachers will want in their classrooms. It is of value as a teaching tool and as personal enrichment for those gray days that come to all.

170 Rubin, Robert Alden, ed., *Poetry Out Loud*, Algonquin Books of Chapel Hill, 1993 (paperback), ISBN 1–56512–122–8, 215 pp., grades 7 and up.

With a memorable introduction by James Earl Jones, this practical volume may become one of the favorite items on the classroom shelf. Jones reveals that poetry became essentially his first means of successful verbal communication as he overcame the hurdle of stuttering. With such an endorsement, reading and writing poetry may gain many new fans—especially among shy or struggling teen communicators.

In this volume Rubin has brought together a mix of traditional and contemporary works that beg to be read aloud or quoted from memory for the sheer pleasure of the sound. With intriguing chapter headings such as "Poems of Love and Wreckage," "Light Verse and Poems that Tell Stories," "Poems of Contradiction and Opposition," "Poems of Vision," and "Art, Poetry, and the Making Thereof," it is obvious that there is something here that may interest almost any reader. Accompanying each poem are marginal notes that enlighten the reader on some interesting facet of the verse, the writer, or the time in which the work was composed. This sort of an intellectual trivia game provides just the kind of information that may give teachers of poetry a new zest for the art.

Variety of approach characterizes this collection. The familiar and comforting "All Things Bright and Beautiful" by Cecil Frances Alexander contrasts with Adreinne Rich's exploration of danger in "Diving into the Wreck." For the reader who loves animals, there is "The Cat as Cat" by Denise Levertov as well as Sir Philip Sidney's "Dear, Why Make You More of a Dog Than Me?" Tribute mingles with despair in Gwendolyn Brooks' "We Real Cool" and tribute with frustration in Edgar Allan Poe's "Sonnet—To Science."

Special features include the marginal notes and additional information given in a section entitled, "Further Notes on the Poems," located at the end of the book. It is almost as if Rubin had commented to his readers in parting, "Oh, yes, and there is one more thing I wanted to say." Such a conclusion is fitting, as the format of this collection is in conversational style with the editor creating an almost "out loud" atmosphere on paper.

171 Rylant, Cynthia, *Soda Jerk*, illus. by Peter Catalanotto, Orchard Books, 1990 (hardcover), ISBN 0–531–05864–6, 47 pp., grades 9 and up.

Working behind the soda counter of Maywells' drugstore gives this nameless young adult an opportunity to observe the flow of life in his small rural town. As inhabitants parade before him, almost as characters in a play, he begins to draw conclusions regarding their lives. The question arises, however, as to whether these poems are about the people of this small town or about the observer himself. The conclusions he draws reveal his own thoughts and feelings as much as those of others, and uncover an underlying thread of loneliness and isolation.

Unique in its format, with double-page watercolor illustrations at the beginning, the end, and sandwiched in between two groups of verse, this volume should appeal to most teens. There is plentiful fodder for group discussion, as the poems touch on many issues pertinent to the age group. The search for self-image and self-expression, the divorce of parents, jealousy of the advantages of other teens, and daydreams for the future all find expression here. Other more universal themes have to do with the death of a grandparent and the attempted suicide of an acquaintance. Overall these twenty-eight poems should find a ready acceptance in the classroom.

172 Rylant, Cynthia, *Something Permanent*, photos by Walker Evans, Harcourt Brace and Company, 1994, (hardcover), ISBN 0–15–277090–9, 61 pp., grades 9 and up.

Working for the Farm Security Administration in the 1930s, Walter Evans documented the effects of the Great Depression on the lives of ordinary people. Twenty-nine of these photos have been "set to poetry" by Cynthia Rylant in *Something Permanent*. Writing as one who has grown up in a similar environment, who knows first hand the story behind the pictures, this poet enhances the reader's understanding of the drama of trouble and suffering portrayed. Photos of empty rooms become peopled in the reader's imagination and are alive with emotional impact.

Some of the titles, like "Gunshop," are jarring. They seem at first reading not to relate to the picture at all. Others, such as "Grave" and "Rocker," feel as though the picture could hardly mean anything else. Though taken in the 1930s, the black and white photos with their accompanying verses are timeless. All is not somber and hopeless in the collection, for a wry humor is injected with "Walls" and "Wash," which treat with dignity the efforts of people to survive in a difficult world. Poems and photos could easily stand alone, but together their impact is powerful. The artful design of the book, with variably placed poems set opposite their accompanying photos in each double-page spread, adds to the enjoyment of the reader. There is no table of contents or index to the twenty-nine pieces of art, but the geographical location of each picture is identified in a section titled "Photographs."

173 Rylant, Cynthia, *Waiting to Waltz: A Childhood*, illus. by Stephen Gammell, Macmillan Books for Young Readers, 1974 (hardcover), ISBN 0–02–778000–7, 47 pp., grades 6 and up.

In this collection of poems, Cynthia Rylant takes the reader into her memory book of experiences growing up in a small town in West Virginia. Beginning at age four, the remembrances stretch on through the adolescent years. No deep desires for escape overshadow these verses, but rather a gentle unveiling of the people who made up her life. Personality quirks are exposed while a sense of respect for individuality is maintained. Appalachian culture is revealed with a sense of appreciation for those who live in the region. Readers looking for the light-hearted humor combined with glimpses of life's serious issues characteristic of the author's works will not be disappointed. Classes reading other works by Ms. Rylant may find these poems add richness to their study.

Though the experiences highlighted cover a span from age four to young adulthood, the issues of death explored in "Forgotten," single-parent families touched on in "The Kool-Kup PTA," and self-discovery expressed in "Band Practice" may be better appreciated by the older student. Whether the surroundings of their youth echo those of the author, many teens will remember the fears, the joys, the yearnings of their growing years and will find themselves saying, "I remember when. . . ." Stephen Gammell's soft and shadowy black and white sketches are a lovely reflection of memories expressed. A table of contents provides the only index to this slim volume.

174 Sandburg, Carl, *Grassroots: Poems*, illus. by Wendell Minor, Browndeer Press, Harcourt Brace Jovanovich, 1998 (hardcover), ISBN 0–15–200082–8, unpaged, grades 6 and up.

The poems selected for this collection of Sandburg's verse are a tribute to the heartland of America. Visual and written images of horses, fields, and harvest times blend to evoke the feel of the Midwest. Broadly arranged by season from spring to late winter, the sixteen poems highlight man's close relationship with and dependence upon the forces of nature. "Buffalo Dusk" speaks to the passing of one era on the prairie, while "Red and White" counters with the ongoing march of the seasons. The full-page watercolors of Wendell Minor, a bright and lovely tribute to our prairie regions, highlight and support Sandburg's verse. Those who have ever known the prairie will hear a call from these artists to celebrate their rural heritage.

175 Sandburg, Carl, *Rainbows Are Made*, selected by Lee Bennett Hopkins, illus. by Fritz Eichenberg, Harcourt Brace Jovanovich, 1982 (hardcover), ISBN 0–15–265480–1, 82 pp., grades 6 and up.

Hopkins has selected short poems and excerpts of longer poems to create an anthology of Carl Sandburg's verses that appeals to young readers. Drawing heavily from "The People, Yes," section one takes a look at the human race with sensitivity and respect. Section two features Sandburg's ability to play with words. In section three ordinary items are shown to signify larger meanings. A "Shirt," for example, becomes an expression of identity. "Pencils" become an integral part of telling a story. "Nature," "The Sea," and "Night" round out the last three divisions of the book with short selections like "Fog," as well as the lengthier "Spring Cries." Each section is set off by one of Sandburg's "Tentative (First Model) Definitions of Poetry" and a wood engraving designed by Fritz Eichenberg. Hopkins' introduction gives helpful background information about Carl Sandburg, and indexes to first lines and titles are found at the back of the book.

176 Schmidt, Gary, ed., *Poetry for Young People: Robert Frost*, illus. by Henri Sorenson, Sterling Publishing Company, 1994 (hardcover), ISBN 0–80969–0633–2, 48 pp., grades 10 and up.

Gary Schmidt and Henri Sorenson have created a small masterpiece in their unified selection and illustration of this lovely volume. With end pages inviting enough to step into, this is a book that seems to invite, "Come with me." The four seasons establish divisions for the twenty-nine poems. Paintings on every page decorate the verses. Special features include a three-page biography of Robert Frost, covering his life from birth in 1874 on through his four Pulitzer Prizes. Perhaps modern readers might even have seen a film clip of his other crowning achievement as he read his poem, "The Gift Outright" at the inauguration of President John F. Kennedy. There are also footnotes for each poem that add helpful explanations that enlarge and enrich the reader's appreciation for these timeless verses. In the chapter entitled "Poems of Summer," Frost makes cleaning a spring seem like a memorable excursion in "The Pasture." Sorenson's illustrations of "Hyla Brook" entice one to go wading. In the "Poems of Autumn," the reader may reflect on "The Road Not Taken." "Poems of Winter" includes a brisk walk in "Good Hours." The year is completed with "Poems of Spring" and two of Frost's frequently quoted compositions, "Birches," and "Mending Wall."

177   Singer, Marilyn, *The Morgans Dream*, illus. by Gary Drake, Henry Holt and Company, 1995 (hardcover), ISBN 0–8050–3004–2, unpaged, grades 6–9.

Gary Drake's dream-like illustrations are a perfect complement to the selections of *The Morgans Dream*. Taking each member of the Morgan family one at a time, the author reveals the bedtime fantasies of each from the grandparents down to the dog. Catherine lives the embarrassment of appearing before her fellow classmates clad only in underwear and boots. Amy's vision of monsters subsides only in her sister's bed. Daisy the dog finds bliss and freedom in romping in the city park. Grandpa dreams of youthful days that for him, can be found in dreams alone. Using a picture book format, this title would provide additional material for a unit on dreams. No index is given or needed for the fifteen poems included.

178   Soto, Gary, *A Fire in My Hands: A Book of Poems*, illus. by James M. Cardillo, Scholastic, 1990 (hardcover), ISBN 0–590–45021–2, 63 pp., grades 10 and up.

Gary Soto invites readers to participate in small episodes of his own life in this warm collection of verses. Although currently professor of English and Chicano studies at the University of California at Berkeley, Soto grew up in less prestigious surroundings. This anthology allows readers to have intimate glimpses into the author's world from his first love to fatherhood. In "Black Hair," Soto confesses his lack of prowess at baseball at eight years of age. Hector Moreno, however gave him a hero with whom to identify and vicariously to taste victory. "How to Sell Things" depicts the psychology of how to approach which neighborhood grandmother and to be almost guaranteed a sale. "Hitchhiking with a Friend and a Book That Explains the Pacific Ocean" may hold the secret to Soto's success as a poet—finding a sense of wonder in all things. The signature work, "Oranges," sheds light on the title of this collection while expressing the poignant angst of first love.

Special features of this memorable volume begin with a foreword written in the first person, drawing the reader into something akin to a dialogue with Soto. Throughout the book there are brief narratives preceding each poem providing a backdrop for the creation of the piece. In conclusion, there is a section called

"Questions and Answers About Poetry" in which the author responds to some common queries relating to his writing. All in all this is a friendly little collection that welcomes young adult readers into the neighborhood—that of poetry and of Mexican life.

179 Soto, Gary, *Neighborhood Odes*, illus. by David Diaz, Harcourt, Brace and Company, 1992 (hardcover), ISBN 0–15–256879–4, 68 pp., grades 6–10.

Soto opens a window for the reader into a Mexican American neighborhood as seen through the eyes of a young child. Finding poetry in sneakers in "Ode to Pablo's Tennis Shoes," ice cream trucks in "Ode of Los Raspados," and in family picnics as portrayed in "Ode of Mi Parques," the author revives childhood memories for readers of all nationalities. With the exception of "Ode to Family Photographs," the verses are short-lined, averaging three to five words per line. Moods vary from poem to poem, reflecting the mercurial emotions of children as they shift from happiness to fear, excitement, and even shame. The black and white illustrations of David Diaz scattered throughout look somewhat like abstract paper-cut designs. Although most of the Spanish words sprinkled here and there are understandable from context, a glossary is found at the back of the book. It may have been more helpful if the words had been translated on the page where they were used.

180 Springer, Nancy, *Music of Their Hooves: Poems About Horses*, illus. by Sandy Rabinowitz, Boyds Mill Press, 1994 (hardcover), ISBN 1–56397–182–8, 32 pp., grades 5 and up.

From workhorses to wild stallions, all types of steeds find a place of honor in Nancy Springer's collection of verse. Twenty poems with settings from country meadows to rugged plains show an understanding of the animal and reveal the love that can exist between horse and rider. Though not full of deep insights, these free verse poems nevertheless are descriptive and cover a variety of the experiences of young horse enthusiasts. Although many of Sandy Rabinowitz's soft and moody watercolor illustrations feature younger children, they effectively complement the verse, which should appeal to horse lovers from two to ninety-two. An index of titles and first lines is included for easy reference.

181 Stafford, William, *Learning to Live in the World: Earth Poems, by William Stafford*, ed. by Jerry Watson and Laura Apol Obbink, Harcourt Brace Jovanovich, 1994 (hardcover), ISBN 0–15–200208–1, 70 pp., grades 7 and up.

Relationships are the point of focus for the fifty poems included in *Learning to Live in the World*. The importance of man's respect for nature and for other people rings loudly through these verses which give glimpses of both the beauty and struggles of life. An ordinary moment becomes an extraordinary event when nature and man connect by such a simple happening as a dandelion puff landing on a shirt sleeve. Guilt from a broken friendship and longing for a companion far away will resonate with readers who have experienced such losses themselves. Complex in implication but accessible in language and tone, these poems will enrich the life of the reader.

182 Strauss, Gwen, *Trail of Stones*, illus. by Anthony Browne, Alfred A. Knopf, 1990 (paperback), ISBN 0–679–90582–0, 35 pp., grades 10 and up.

Folklore collection, picture book, poetry anthology all describe this medley by Gwen Strauss. Each of the twelve pieces looks into the heart of a character already known to readers through fairy tales. Anthony Browne's stark black and white illustrations create the perfect accompaniment for the tale told. Hansel and Gretel's father reveals the motivation behind the apparent cowardice in his abandonment of his children in "Their Father." Readers may wonder about the ultimate fate of Snow White after reading "Confessions of a Witch." The possibility that the wife of a king does not always live happily ever after is explored in "Her Shadow." Although some of the verses include sinister suggestions and adult allusions to sex, the discerning teacher will find selections in this small collection that provide a stimulating introduction to folk literature. Each verse takes an introspective look at a familiar character, which may encourage students to light their own imaginative spark through creative writing.

183 Sullivan, Charles, ed. *Imaginary Gardens: American Poetry and Art for Young People*, Harry N. Abrams, 1989 (hardcover), ISBN 0–8109–1130–2, 105 pp., grades 7 and up.

In the introduction to this collection, Charles Sullivan expresses, in a candidly personal note, his passionate desire for his audience to enjoy the truth of poetry. One might even say it was the brainchild of Talking Heads. Sullivan reveals that the idea for this work was born after he had read the lyrics from a tape he had bought for his son. In listening and reading those lyrics, Sullivan recognized a form of poetry that expressed universal and age-spanning emotions, and he wished to capture the same feelings through the medium of classic art and literature.

Visual arts share equal billing with poetic phrases as the editor offers to young adults the opportunity to connect life with aesthetic experiences. Writers included represent a wide range of time and topic from Marianne Moore to Shel Silverstein. Artists also have been chosen to represent a breadth of styles—from Matthew Brady's photographs to Grandma Moses' landscapes.

Walt Whitman's "The Place Where a Great City Stands" reminds readers what aspects of life supply strength in urban areas. "High Flight," by John Gillespie Magee, Jr., inspires future leaders with the thrill of space exploration. Mary Austin's translation of "A Song of Greatness" rings with the pride of the Chippewa people. Shel Silverstein pays tribute to the cultural phenomenon of contemporary music in "Rock 'n Roll Band." Within this varied collection of poetry and art, there should be something that strikes the cord of truth in every reader.

184 Turner, Ann, *Grass Songs*, illus. by Barry Moser, Harcourt Brace Jovanovich, 1993 (hardcover), ISBN 0–15–136788–4, 51 pp., grades 10 and up.

Giving more than historical facts, Ann Turner reveals the thoughts and passions, joys and sorrows, of the women who made the trek in covered wagons across the American prairies and mountains to the promised land of the Pacific Coast. Taking information from the journals of real pioneer women, Turner has worked to recapture their lives, to tell the stories of those who rejoiced in the freedom obtained and those who grieved in the losses suffered. The tremendous physical and emotional cost paid by these brave women is clearly revealed in "No Time Enough" and "Raspberry Graves." The conflicting loyalties of a woman taken by the Indians then later returned to white civilization are made clear in "Olive Oatman." Barry Moser's stunning pencil sketches based on historical photographs flesh out the seventeen word pictures.

185 Turner, Ann, *A Lion's Hunger: Poems of First Love*, illus. by Maria Jimenez, Marshall Cavendish, 1998 (hardcover), ISBN 0–7614–5035–1, 47 pp., grades 10 and up.

In only forty-seven pages, Turner and Jimenez vividly express the impact of first love. Sparse narrative, reminiscent of journal writing, gives an air of intimacy to the work, which is enhanced by dated entries and the personal touch of an attached ribbon to serve as a bookmark. The odyssey, for that is what it seems to be, begins in September, when boy meets girl. Written from a first person perspective, the verses reveal the gradual unfolding of a dating relationship that seems to exclude all other people in the world. Appetite, communication with parents, classes in school, all pale in comparison. In April there is an automobile accident as the result of weather and wine. Parents impose restrictions. Love fades. By July both teens are seeing other people and eventually the narrator finds herself whole again—without a male to define her very being.

The "lion's hunger" of the title expresses the consuming need for that significant other in the soul of a teen. The poignancy of love found, lost, and a new life established in the wake of a broken heart speaks powerfully to the young adult audience. The eight portrait-quality illustrations capture the mood of the text as surely as photographs would reflect the pages in a diary. Although both teens remain anonymous throughout the book, Jimenez provides faces and expressions so realistic that the reader feels as if she knows them. Readers of all ages who have experienced the bittersweet pangs of first love will be reminded that life goes on, even when love doesn't. The young person who believes that finding love is the answer to all life's problems will discover that any commitment of the heart always involves risk.

186 Watson, Esther Pearl, and Mark Todd, *The Pain Tree*, illus. by Esther Pearl Watson and Mark Todd, Houghton Mifflin, 2000 (paperback), ISBN 0–618–01558–2, 62 pp., grades 10 and up.

Watson and Todd scoured web sites and magazines such as *react* and *Seventeen* to find the twenty-five selections for their anthology of poetry written by and for teens. Subjects covered are those one would expect to find in this type of volume—the search for identity and acceptance, fears about the future, and the vagaries of love. Young adult insecurity and the fear of rejection are the message of "In My Mind." "Nervous" describes the emotional roller coaster of hope and disappointment produced by the physical proximity of someone who is the object of desire. Asserting a personal identity against the pull of the crowd is the theme of "Thoughts of the Different." Finally, the ultimate desire of all, to be seen as a person of worth, is the thrust of "Not a Doll," and "Waste of Time."

Each poem is accompanied by a full-page illustration done in bold, bright colors and a childlike abstract format. Pictures to portray the poems written by males were done by Mark Todd. Esther Watson designed pages to illustrate those verses written by females. The paintings are melodramatic and at times portray more angst than the poems warrant.

The literary quality of the poems included is not consistent. This may be explained by the statements in the section titled "The Poets," where quotations from the authors give insight into their motivations for writing. Numerous contributors cited poetry as a means of working through difficult times, releasing bottled up feelings, or alleviating dark moods. Teens who are searching for a way to express their own frustrations, or who desire to voice an understanding they have reached in their own life, may find inspiration here. "Words from the Artists" at the front of the book and "The Artists" page at the back explain the compilers' motivation in producing the anthology.

187 Wayant, Patricia, ed., *Think Positive Thoughts Every Day*, Blue Mountain Press, 1999 (paperback), ISBN 0–88396–466–X, unpaged, grades 8 and up.

In an introductory essay, Regina Hill sets the tone for this volume, as she impresses upon readers the importance of attitude in facing life and establishing relationships. Each verse and prose piece in the anthology expresses a variation of this theme encouraging optimism. Ben Daniels gives suggestions on what to do and what not to do in "Motto for a Positive Outlook." Deanna Beisser extols the virtue of dreams in "Promise Yourself Only the Best." Nancye Sims issues her challenge in "You Can Make Something Happy Out of Everything That Happens in Life." Miniature illustrations in soft colors are sprinkled randomly throughout the book. Pastel and white pages alternate to provide an overall feeling of gentleness. Printed on sturdy, recycled paper, this small collection will create a bright spot on any library shelf. The only special feature is the closing acknowledgments page.

188 Willard, Nancy, coll., *Step Lightly: Poems for the Journey*, Harcourt, Brace and Company, 1998 (hardcover), ISBN 0–15–201849–2, 112 pp., grades 9 and up.

The "journey" begins with Emily Dickinson's predawn "Will There Really Be A 'Morning'?" and concludes with "Who Is the East?" by the same author as she bids adieu to the sun. In between are the ordinary events and creatures that make a day as seen through the extraordinary eyes of poets, both classic and contemporary. What ties this collection together is simply that these are favorites of the compiler, Nancy Willard, who had clipped and saved these verses in a shoebox over a period of many years. However, there is a unity of life about them as seen through time, the seasons, animals, and relationships.

In this anthology for young adults, Willard pays tribute to her audience by offering works traditionally considered fare for the more experienced in life. This is not a young adult collection, but rather an adult collection that may be *enjoyed* by young adults. Variety in topic and writer reflects what might be an interesting trek through any twenty-four-hour period. James Wright ponders the future of a babe in "Mutterings Over the Crib of a Deaf Child." Alexis Rotella steps inside the mind of a small child-artist in "Purple." Radcliffe Squires steps outside to wonder at the gentleness of "Snow." Valerie Linet makes versifying concrete in "Poetry Loaves." Denise Levertov expresses the urgency of putting words on paper in "Writing in the Dark." This is just a sample of the forty contributors that span centuries and continents. In a conversational introduction Willard shares how the book came about and suggests ways that the reader may best respond to it. She closes with brief biographical sketches of the authors in "Notes on the Poets."

189 Wong, Janet, *Behind the Wheel: Poems About Driving*, Margaret K. McElderry Books, 1999 (hardcover), ISBN 0–689–82531–5, 44 pp., grades 10 and up.

Janet Wong approaches the whole ordeal of learning to drive through the eyes of the young adult in the driver's seat. Readers who may be familiar with

Wong's earlier works, *The Rainbow Hand: Poems About Mothers and Children,* *A Suitcase of Seaweed and Other Poems,* and *Good Luck Gold and Other Poems* should find this collection equally intriguing. Although her heritage is Chinese and Korean, Wong's free verse stanzas are neither socially nor culturally bound. One can imagine any teen reader thinking, "Yeah, if I could write poetry, this is what I would say."

As varied in subject as cars on the freeway vary in style, these brief verses cover topics ranging from getting a license to being pulled over by the police. "Hard on the Gas" reminiscences on the speed-up then slow-down pace of a ride with Grandpa. "Insurance for Teenage Drivers: A New Plan" poses a nearly foolproof method of limiting traffic violations to two per person. "Stuff" reminds the young person what to do when there is trouble on the road. "You Have Got To" may cause the less cautious young driver to consider the fact that there *is* a tomorrow. Many young drivers will find that Wong speaks for them as she addresses parents, grandparents, policeman, and peers. Having read her realistic verses, the novice may check the back seat the next time he gets behind the wheel, just to see if Ms. Wong has been riding there all along.

190 Wong, Janet S., *Good Luck Gold and Other Poems,* Margaret K. McElderry Books, 1994 (hardcover), ISBN 0–689–50617–1, 42 pp., grades 5 and up.

For a young person who has grown up in a Chinese-American setting, these poems describe experiences they know well. For others, they provide an introduction to the Asian-American community that moves beyond stereotype. Whether speaking of family in "Grandmother's Cure," food in "Deli Circus," or cultural heritage in "Bound Feet," the ethnicity is strongly personal and yet the pain of bigotry experienced in "Waiting at the Railroad Café" rings universal. The confusion of identity caused by moving between two cultures finds vent in "All Mixed-Up," and a determination to be seen as an individual apart from cultural background comes through in "Math." Short and easy to read, this combination of rhymed and free verse, haiku and cinquain, should appeal to a large age group. If combined with selections from *I Am the Darker Brother* and *Many Winters,* they could form the basis for challenging classroom discussion.

191 Wong, Janet S., *Night Garden: Poems from the World of Dreams,* illus. by Julie Paschkis, Margaret K. McElderry Books, 2000 (hardcover), ISBN 0–689–82617–6, 28 pp., grades 6–10.

Anyone who has ever dreamed can find at least one poem in Janet Wong's *Night Garden* that will strike a cord in memory. The two-toned diptych illustrations have a surrealistic look that is often associated with a dream state. "Whose Face Is This?" suggests that the self we see in dreams may be closer to reality than the one we hide behind a mask when awake. Dreams of falling, flying, speaking fluently in an unknown language, and the unavoidable nightmare fill out the pages. Short and lively, these fifteen poems should have special appeal to the younger adult.

192 Wong, Janet S., *A Suitcase of Seaweed and Other Poems*, illus. by the author, Margaret K. McElderry Books, 1996 (hardcover), ISBN 0–689–80788–0, 42 pp., grades 6–10.

Janet Wong uses the experiences of her own life to weave a poetic tapestry reconciling three different cultures. The first section reveals the influence of her Korean mother's ancestry in verses titled "Acupuncture," "Rice Cooker," and the signature poem, "A Suitcase of Seaweed." Her Chinese heritage comes into play in "Tea Ceremony" and "After a Dinner of Fish." The confusion of blending these separate backgrounds with her American identity is clearly expressed in "Manners" and "Which?" Readers from many ethnic backgrounds will recognize the various kinds of prejudice encountered by the author. They may gain courage from vicarious participation in her struggles to respect her heritage while she forged her own sense of personhood. The thirty-six short poems are accessed through the table of contents.

193 Wood, Nancy, ed., *Many Winters: Prose and Poetry of the Pueblos*, illus. by Frank Howell, Doubleday Books for Young Readers, 1974 (paperback), ISBN 0–385–30865–5, 80 pp., grades 9 and up.

A reverence for Native American culture and an appreciation for the wisdom of elders shine through this anthology of poetry and prose of the Pueblo Indians. The exquisite, detailed paintings of Frank Howell strengthen this respect. They show more than facial features. They reveal the soul of his subjects. The selections chosen by Ms. Wood for inclusion record the unique way of life of the Taos Pueblo and their vision of the world. A quality of contentment runs like a quiet river through verses like "When I Look at Ugliness, I See Beauty." An understanding of the earth and the ways of nature is expressed in "The Earth Is All That Lasts." "Many Moons I Have Lived" declares an acceptance of the passage of time. There is no searching for identity here, but a knowing of one's self that should give reassurance to young adults. They should also feel challenged by the charge that is left to them in "Hold On to What Is Good."

194 Woolger, David, comp. *Who Do You Think You Are? Poems About People*, Oxford University Press, 1990 (hardcover), ISBN 0–19–276074–2, 128 pp., grades 8 and up.

Drawing from more than eighty writers and five artists, David Woolger presents his unique approach to Who's Who. Spanning hundreds of years from the eighth century to contemporary writers and crossing cultural boundaries, Woolger presents a parade of personalities in verse. Each selection focuses on some facet of being human.

The 113 poems are divided into ten chapters with titles that categorize the groupings. Chapter 3, "Young and Old," lists selections from such extreme stages of life as "Childhood" by Frances Cornford and "How to Be Old" by May Swenson. Chapter 7, "Silences and Words (Sometimes, Poetry)," includes Carl Sandburg's warning on the use of proud words in "Primer Lesson," while Sheika A El-Miskery observes the significance of silence in "Just A Word." Chapters 8 and 9, entitled, respectively, "Solitudes" and "Connections," each contain verses dealing with life experienced alone and in a social setting. Samples of other chapter titles are "A World of Different People," "The Peerless and the Skilled," and "Feeling Bad—Then Feeling Good."

Special features include indexes of poets, artists, titles, and first lines. Acknowledgments pages identify sources for each selection. A scattering of pen and ink sketches by a variety of artists complement the verses. Although not compiled especially for a young adult audience, selections from this anthology will be well received by young readers as they struggle with identity issues and the complexities of understanding others.

195 Worth, Valerie, *all the small poems*, illus. by Natalie Babbitt, Farrar, Straus and Giroux, 1987 (paperback), ISBN 0–374–40344–9, 173 pp., grades 6 and up.

Award winning writer Valerie Worth has brought together between the covers of this book a collection of collections. Included are four of her previous works—*small poems, more small poems, still more small poems*, and *small poems again*. The repetitions in the titles is not an indication of limited originality but rather demonstrates how Worth uses simple things to speak profoundly. Natalie Babbitt's understated pen and ink sketches offer quiet accompaniment to each piece.

The nearly one hundred verses provide unique perspectives on common aspects of life. "pebbles" (poem titles lowercase to match original publication) reminds readers of why collecting stones carries with it the anticipation of a treasure hunt. "acorn" expresses the awe one feels in observing the potential for greatness lying dormant in the capped nut. "compass" shrinks the immensity of the world into the palm of a hand. With a few lines of free verse, Worth demonstrates her ability to take delight in those aspects of life that seem most mundane. Young adults will find special joy in this collection as they view common objects with the poet's sense of wonder. There will be *some* animal, item, or place, that will speak to every reader, whether it be a "door," or a "coat hanger," or "garbage" or. . . .

196 Yolen, Jane, *O Jerusalem*, illus. by John Thompson, Blue Sky Press, 1996 (hardcover), ISBN 0–590–48426–5, unpaged, grades 7 and up.

Perhaps there is no more turbulent city in the world than Jerusalem. Jane Yolen and John Thompson have captured the passion of this place on paper—in poetry, prose, and illustration. Yolen balances the feelings and faith of all three religions—Jewish, Christian, and Muslim—that lay claim to this hallowed ground. Thompson captures a range of moods in majestic acrylic paintings supporting each page of text.

In "Dome of the Rock" readers grasp in four stanzas the division and unity of the hallowed site. "Tokens from Jerusalem" poses the question of what will be left of the city itself if each pilgrim takes what he wants from the land. "Jerusalem 3000" looks with hope to the future for peace in the city whose name (one of seventy) echoes that promise. Young adults who witness scenes of violence almost nightly on televised news will have a deeper understanding of the significance of the Holy City after reading this book.

Yolen gives special helps throughout the volume. "About Jerusalem" introduces the text. Prose sections provide factual information that deepens the meaning of each poem. On the final page, the author shares her hope for a future of peace in an afterward.

197 Yolen, Jane, *Water Music*, photo. by Jason Stemple, Wordsong/Boyds Mill Press, 1995 (hardcover), ISBN 1–56397–336–7, 40 pp., grades 6 and up.

Inspired by the choice photographs of Jason Stemple, Yolen has composed seventeen verses built around a water theme. Though many are simple enough for a child to understand, most are thoughtful enough to give pause to the adult. All promote an attitude of quiet contemplation. The author is able to put words to the feelings that arise in the human heart when observing the beauty and power of this basic element of nature.

The layout features one poem in large print, attractively arranged to complement the photo positioned on each two-page spread. With verses that encourage an understanding of the ways water profoundly affects all aspects of life, science teachers may find the collection supportive of projects that encourage writing across the curriculum.

198 Zolotow, Charlotte, *River Winding*, illus. by Kazue Mizumura, Thomas Y. Crowell, 1970 (hardcover), ISBN 0–690–03867–4, unpaged, grades 6–9.

These twenty-two unsophisticated poems by Charlotte Zolotow, express an appreciation of nature and the changing seasons. Short in length, they distill the essence of man's interaction with the world around him into a few poignant lines. Easy enough for a child to understand, they are substantive enough to cause the adult to reflect upon the joy of life's simple moments. The comfort of a dog nuzzling the hand brings relief from loneliness in "A Dog." "The Sandpiper" evokes memories of lazy days on the beach in summer. Readers can vicariously feel the cold as they read "River in Winter." The gently expressive two-color paintings by Kazue Mizumura match the poetry well. There are short biographical sketches of the author and illustrator. No index is provided, but one is not really needed for this diminutive work.

Thematic Guide to Poems

(Numerals refer to bibliography entry numbers. Titles in quotation marks are poems that can be found within the corresponding entry.)

relief

religion

Index of Writers with Book Titles

(Numerals refer to bibliography entry numbers.)

Nash, Ogden, comp., *The Moon Is Shining Bright as Day*, 148

Norman, Gurney, ed. *See* Baber, no. 15.

Nye, Naomi Shihab, and Paul B. Janeczko, eds., *I Feel a Little Jumpy Around You*, 149

Nye, Naomi Shihab, comp., *Salting the Ocean: 100 Poems by Young Poets*, 150

Nye, Naomi Shihab, comp., *The Space Between Our Footsteps: Poems and Paintings from the Middle East*, 151

Nye, Naomi Shihab, comp., *This Same Sky: A Collection of Poems from Around the World*, 152

Nye, Naomi Shihab, comp., *The Tree Is Older Than You Are: A Bilingual Gathering of Poems and Stories from Mexico with Paintings by Mexican Artists*, 153

Nye, Naomi Shihab, ed., *what have you lost?*, 154

Okutoro, Lydia Omolola, comp., *Quiet Storm: Voices of Young Black Poets*, 155

Panzer, Nora, ed., *Celebrate America in Poetry and Art*, 156

Paulos, Martha, comp., *Felines: Great Poets on Notorious Cats*, 157

Paulos, Martha, ed. and illus., *insectAsides*, 158

Peck, Richard, ed., *Mindscapes: Poems for the Real World*, 159

Peck, Richard, ed., *Sounds and Silences*, 160

Perkins, Agnes, comp. *See* Hill, no. 67.

Philip, Neil, ed., *Singing America: Poems That Define a Nation*, 161

Philip, Neil, ed., *War and the Pity of War*, 162

Plotz, Helen, comp., *Imagination's Other Place: Poems of Science and Mathematics*, 163

Pollinger, Ginn, sel., *Something Rich and Strange: A Treasury of Shakepeare's Verse*, 164

Ray, David, and Judy Ray, eds., *Fathers: A Collection of Poems*, 165

Ray, Judy, ed. *See* Ray, no. 165.

Robertson, Barbara, comp. *See* Downie, no. 31.

Rogansky, Barbara, ed., *Winter Poems*, 166

Rosenberg, Liz, ed., *Earth-Shattering Poems*, 167

Rosenberg, Liz, ed., *The Invisible Ladder*, 168

Rosenberg, Liz, ed., *Light-Gathering Poems*, 169

Rubin, Robert Alden, ed., *Poetry Out Loud*, 170

Rylant, Cynthia, *Soda Jerk*, 171

Rylant, Cynthia, *Something Permanent*, 172

Rylant, Cynthia, *Waiting to Waltz: A Childhood*, 173

Sandburg, Carl, *Grassroots: Poems*, 174

Sandburg, Carl, D. *Rainbows Are Made*, 175

Schmidt, Gary, D. ed., *Poetry for Young People: Robert Frost*, 176

Singer, Beverly R., ed. *See* Hirschfelder, no. 68.

Singer, Marilyn, *The Morgans Dream*, 177

Smith, Hugh, comp. *See* Dunning, nos. 33, 34.

Soto, Gary, *A Fire in My Hands: A Book of Poems*, 178

Soto, Gary, *Neighborhood Odes*, 179

Springer, Nancy, *Music of Their Hooves: Poems About Horses*, 180

Stafford, William, *Learning to Live in the World: Earth Poems*, 181

Strauss, Gwen, *Trail of Stones*, 182

Stuart-Clark, Christopher, comp./ed. *See* Harrison, nos. 62, 63.

Sullivan, Charles, ed., *Imaginary Gardens: American Poetry and Art for Young People*, 183

Swenson, May, ed. *See* Knudson, no. 105.

Turner, Ann, *Grass Songs*, 184

Turner, Ann, *A Lion's Hunger: Poems of First Love*, 185

Watson, Esther Pearl, and Mark Todd, *The Pain Tree*, 186

Wayant, Patricia, ed., *Think Positive Thoughts Every Day*, 187

Willard, Nancy, coll., *Step Lightly: Poems for the Journey*, 188

Wilson, Edward E., comp. *See* Carroll, no. 24.

Wong, Janet S., *Behind the Wheel: Poems About Driving*, 189

Wong, Janet S., *Good Luck Gold and Other Poems*, 190

Wong, Janet S., *Night Garden: Poems from the World of Dreams*, 191

Wong, Janet S., *A Suitcase of Seaweed and Other Poems*, 192

Wood, Nancy, ed., *Many Winters: Prose and Poetry of the Pueblos*, 193

Woolger, David, comp., *Who Do You Think You Are?: Poems About People*, 194

Worth, Valerie, *all the small poems*, 195

Yolen, Jane, *O Jerusalem*, 196

Yolen, Jane, *Water Music*, 197

Zolotow, Charlotte, *River Winding*, 198

Index of Book Titles

Index of Illustrators

(Numerals refer to bibliography entry numbers.)

Index of Other Significant Items

(Numerals refer to bibliography entry numbers.)

About the Authors

RACHEL SCHWEDT is Director of the Curriculum Library at Liberty University. She has previously been an elementary and high school librarian. She and Janice DeLong frequently speak at teachers' conventions regarding the use of literature in the classroom.

JANICE DELONG currently serves on the faculty of Liberty University where she teaches children's literature. She supervises student teachers on both public and private school campuses. She has been a classroom teacher in primary, elementary, and middle schools.